INTIMACY EXPOSED   Toilet, Bathroom, Restroom   Edited by Javier Fernández Contreras and Roberto Zancan

ISSUE I

INTIMACY EXPOSED

Intimacy Exposed
An Introduction to the Study of Toilets, Bathrooms, Restrooms
Javier Fernández Contreras and Roberto Zancan

"Toilet" is a euphemism, the fruit of a figure of speech more than a metonymy. In contemporary Western societies, this ultimate area of privacy received its name in a process of extension and social exchange. Our social need for polite, indirect expressions to designate a place dedicated to evacuation in a public context (e.g. trains, buildings, and urban parks) transformed what was initially a piece of fabric into an item of furniture, then into a room, and finally into a place filled with other things. It was only once the facility was placed in a room that the *"petite toile"*—the lace-lined linen resting on a shelf where vases, brushes, and any other items required for personal hygiene were placed—became a "toilet".

Because of this transition from a two-dimensional item to an object, then a room, and finally an environment— which often acts as a meeting place—the toilet is a formidable tool to reflect on the current circumstances of interior architecture. It is useful in describing the private and collective features of past and present health, sexual, clinical, and hygienic appliances. It is also a place where we can understand the exchanges between individuals and communities, subjects and behavior, and even between bacterial-plant-animal organisms and humankind.

In its varied shapes and sizes, the toilet addresses the obscurity of the relationship between body and space. The persistence of the French term, even in distant cultural contexts, reflects its connection with the process of affirmation of personal hygiene imposed by modernization. As a portmanteau word, the toilet has traveled the world. Occasionally, it returns and shows both proximity and distance from its aristocratic-bourgeois origin. This

1   A paraphrase of the famous "Yet Another Effort, Frenchmen, If You Would Become Republicans", from the fifht dialogue of Marquis de Sade, *La philosophie dans le boudoir*, 1795.

journey through manners, meanings, and locations has also gradually produced an extension of the toilet to incorporate various objects, places, and spaces. *Antibagno* (Italian), *boudoir* (French) and closet (English) are just three examples of the many environments where the toilet has extended its domain over time.

The closer we look at the toilet, the more it looks at us from afar. The more we sit on it, the more we think of the world. It was in the boudoir that the Marquis de Sade drafted his most radical manifesto and his philosophical discourse on freedom, morals, and revolutionary religion: "Yet Another *Push*, Frenchmen, If You Would Become Republicans." (1) Architectural space is not indifferent to this. Manfredo Tafuri evoked the Sadian pamphlet to entitle his famous article on the radicalization of the political interpretation of architecture, *L'Architecture dans le boudoir*.

An analysis of sanitary and others spaces dedicated to personal care, a privacy observatory as it were, helps to assess social changes in depth and decide how we can intervene to directly improve the everyday lives of today's users, how to tackle and resolve conflicts of use between individuals of different sexes and ages in public places, how to raise the quality of public and private health and increase the comfort of housing, work, and leisure. Observing these issues, we are prompted to explore the forms and meanings of bathrooms and private spaces in relation to their different functions, including their use as transgressive and informal meeting places and places of inevitable, forced social coexistence, with a view to transforming these issues into crucial aspects in the disciplines of design and interior architecture. Recently

2   Tala Burki, "Dirt: The Filthy Reality of Everyday Life," *The Lancet Infectious Diseases*, vol. 11, no. 6, 2011.   3   Irma Boom et al., *Elements of Architecture: Toilet,* vol. 11 (Venice: Marsilio Editori, 2014).   4   Museum of London, "Fatberg! Exhibiting the 'Monster of Whitechapel'," https:// www.museumoflondon.org.uk/ discover/exhibiting-fatberg-monster-whitechapel, accessed June 5, 2018.   5   Charlotte Jones, Jen Slater, *Around the Toilet: a research project report about what makes a safe and accessible toilet space* (Sheffield: Sheffield Hallam University, 2018).   6   Francesca Davis Di Piazza, *Remaking the John: the Invention and Reinvention of the Toilet* (Minneapolis: Lerner Publishing Group, 2014).

they have been the focus of several scientific contributions and exhibitions such as *Dirt: The Filthy Reality of Everyday Life* at the Wellcome London Collection in 2011, (2) the *Toilet* display section in *Elements of Architecture* at the Biennale di Architettura di Venezia 2014 curated by Rem Koolhaas, (3) *Fatberg* at the Museum of London in 2018, (4) the Sheffield Hallam University's study, *About the toilet: a research project report about what makes a safe and accessible toilet space (2015–2018),* (5) books like *Remaking the John: The Invention and Reinvention of the Toilet* by Francesca Davis Di Piazza, (6) and many others listed in the annotated bibliography at the end of this volume.

This book takes a new step in this field of research with a series of scientific and artistic interventions, starting with an evaluation of the diversion of uses of "wet areas" in social life, contemplating the evolution of the use of furniture, in order to understand the forms and meanings of details and objects in domestic bathrooms and public toilets. The buildings, environments, events, stories, artistic expressions, and case studies presented here show how necessary it still is to highlight the nature of certain daily needs, still hidden despite their crucial role in our lives. They show that looking at society's evolution in the most intimate aspects of human life is not only a way to comprehend our needs better, but also a way to protect them from misunderstanding and control. In this sense, the hypothesis presented herein is that the analysis of places of intimacy reveals architectural postures as well as unexpected uses, and facilitates the development of new proposals which can generate relevant working suggestions for better solutions for the needs of an increasingly complex and multi-ethnic future society.

This consideration of studies and projects on the subject aims to resume an adjourned "state of the art" on the issues concerning the use and design of spaces for personal hygiene and to relaunch a specific area of expertise in which the Department of Interior Architecture at the Higher School of Art and Design (HEAD) in Geneva could be a center for discussions about these arguments.

The texts in this volume, largely written for the December 2018 seminar entitled "Intimacy Exposed: Toilet, Bathroom, Restroom" (organized by the Department of Interior Architecture at HEAD – Genève to cover a diversity of fields) present a practice-based study of the recent past of modernist technologies and a vision of the future of personal and collective practices regarding the realm of the toilet. (7) Multiple forms of knowledge are gathered here in an applied type of research that uses design, projects, creativity, and artistic expression as tools to investigate and interpret social and functional problems and produce concrete, "liveable", three-dimensional, tangible solutions for these problems. In this context, an international scientific meeting was a methodological choice as a first step to address the research topic. The seminar brought various perspectives on the theme to the fore and produced a critical discussion in a dynamic social event. Divided into separate sections, it brought together those who have conducted research on the subject or have played a consolidated role in the production of knowledge in the fields of physical intimacy and health with less consolidated or emerging experts—selected on the

7   Jean-Pierre Greff, Lysianne Léchot Hirt and Anne-Catherine Sutermeister, "Les défis de la recherche en art et en design en Suisse. Un cas d'école: la HEAD – Genève," Hermès, *La Revue* 72, no. 2 (Paris: C.N.R.S. Editions, 2015): 75–84, https://doi.org/10.3917/herm.072.0075, accessed June 5, 2018.

basis of an open call for contributions—including young researchers, PhD students, and emerging artists, all of whom were interested in questioning the space of health and personal care and had already published research on the topic. The seminar was funded on the basis of equal gender participation.

This book reflects the diversity and complementarity of the seminar participants: museum curators, mass media journalists, art gallery owners, filmmakers, design researchers specializing in resolving gender and health problems, historians, architects, and builders. The research presented at the seminar was an opportunity to share fundamental data about new and little-explored scientific experiments, crossing different disciplinary and epistemological perspectives. From the design perspective, with discussion centered on interior architecture, the seminar produced critical debates about the need to develop spatial situations that cancel the problems of sexual segregation, responses to new needs for intimate places in collective buildings, and new functions to make the toilet space safe and accessible to all in terms of age, social conditions, etc.

For an overview of what is discussed in the book, Alexandra Midal, professor of design history and theory at HEAD – Genève, questions the symbolism of plumbing. Starting with a comparison between Marcel Duchamp's urinal bought in a shop and Le Corbusier's bidet, taken from a catalog of industrial sanitary ware, she goes so far as to demonstrate how sexual manipulations of aesthetic objects and furniture in 20th century art could explain the eradication of women by modernists in the history

8   Joel Sanders, *Stud: Architectures of Masculinity* (New York: Princeton Architectural Press, 1996).

of design and architecture. Philippe Rahm, an architect patiently involved in environmental thinking, presents the case of the construction of an avant-garde system of public services as the conception of gradation of intimacy. He looks at the construction of nine toilets in Taichung's Central Park in Taiwan, which proceeds from a dissociation of layers of protection and perception, each one shifting from outside to inside, creating a concentric circle of boundaries from the most public to the most private that define limits relating to the ground, the light, the sound, taking shelter from the rain, and views. Michael Jakob, professor of history of architecture at HEAD–Genève, analyzes some historical examples of 20th century art and architecture to highlight the ambiguities of toilets, considered as social constructions. He describes the processes that relate to what happens on the inside in a dialectical system that regulates the relationship between the inside and the outside, the pure and the impure, in toilet interiors.

In "From Stud to Stalled! Social Equity and Public Restrooms", Joel Sanders, adjunct professor at Yale University, New Haven, traces the evolution of two decades of work on gender, identity, and design since the publication of his book, *STUD: Architectures of Masculinity*. (8) His essay looks at shifting cultural conceptions about masculinity, femininity, and LBGTQ rights over the past 20 years. Sanders presents "Stalled!", a design research project that takes American controversies about transgender access to public restrooms as a departure point to create inclusive public restrooms that meet the needs of people of different ages, genders, religions, and di-

sabilities. Sanders treats the public restroom as a case study: one example of the way designers can make a difference by exploring the design consequences of urgent social justice issues when human rights are in peril in the United States and around the world. Musing on the many meanings and themes associated with the highly intimate and domestic places that are toilets, bathrooms, and restrooms, the famous and multi-award winning filmmakers Louise Lemoine and Ila Bêka address the various ways their own work explores and translates physical, and by extension psychological, intimacy into images. Renaud Haerlingen addresses recent toilet-related work by Rotor as well as Rotor Deconstruction's current research, which focuses on up-scaling the refurbishment of re-use toilets. The field reports range from toilets stripped from an office building, a toilet project with a sort of Japanese culture around bathing attitude for a community center, toilets from the decommissioned IOC headquarters, toilets from a luxury residence in Gland, and toilets from the hospital in Prato. Catherine Ince, Chief Curator at the Victoria and Albert Museum of London, presents the intriguing history of one of the most extraordinary objects in the V&A's collection: an avant-garde glass bathroom designed in 1932 by the artist Paul Nash, commissioned by surrealist art patron Edward James for his wife Tilly Losch, an Austrian dancer and film star. Her reflection shows how this complex object exemplifies the pursuit of a Gesamtkunstwerk attitude and the progressive spirit of architectural and interior design ideas at play in the thirties, and questions the conservation and exhibition criteria of contemporary museum.

In "*Hygiène populaire*", Mariana Siracusa, founder and curator of SPAZIO Gallery in Milan, wonders about the way in which toilets can be transformed into subjects to create very appealing exhibitions. The toilet is certainly a successful subject: although it is linked to the naked sexualized body and its associated social conventions, we have all gotten used to peeping into the private lives of others. Curators take advantage of the public's voyeuristic inclinations to stretch the topic, include historically-relevant material, and develop a reflection on contemporary design. Should a possible exhibition actually take place in an architecture gallery in Milan, the curator might start the narrative in the 1970s by showing plans of a "*casa a ballatoio*" (public housing) and a Gabriele Basilico photograph of a latrine in the same building. This somewhat disturbing yet familiar picture (for the Italian public) would provide a good starting point for the exhibition to show how much things have changed, in architectural and social terms, to get to the white free-standing bathtubs advertised in so many contemporary magazines.

Eva Gil Lopesino, founder of the Elii architecture office in Madrid, Spain, analyzes some of her projects, and their development of the idea that our everyday lives are like a soap opera. Consequently, spaces like toilets and bathrooms have been designed like a transformable stage, enabled for the choreography, rehearsal, action, and fiction of daily life. These spaces are equipped to intensify the performing experience of the users' bodies, to probe and question their social roles and limits, rehearse their shared imagery, test their subjectivity and explore the potential of the ordinary.

In "Dawn the hall to the right? A glimpse into Le Corbusier's bathrooms", Andrés García Pruñonosa, an architect graduate from the Universitat Politècnica de València, conducts an in-depth analysis of the elements of bathrooms in a series of 20th century homes from a transversal perspective on the architectural work of Le Corbusier and other relevant modernist architects, focusing on their spatial impact on the overall layout of the home. He shows how domestic devices, seemingly restricted to their functional scope, are actually crucial in the organization of the domestic layout.

In the context of society's incipient comprehension of hygienic objectives as a necessity, the bathroom not only emerged as a space for experimentation, but probably also appears as the main contribution to the domestic program of the avant-garde. In addition to these texts, the main contributions to the seminar, this book adds a couple of others essays written for the *Spot on. Toilettengeschichten* exhibition at the Kulturzentrum Alte Fabrik, *Gebert Stiftung für Kultur* Foundation in Rapperswil, from 24 August to 13 October 2019. Although this event was completely independent of the seminar, the connection between the two events is instrumental and not accidental. The small extraordinary exhibition curated by Josiane Imhasly is probably the most interesting recent interpretation of contemporary artistic production around the theme of toilets, as confirmed by her essays. So somehow, precisely due to the fact that initially there was no relationship between the two events, this has been an indirect confirmation of the interest in the research theme, further confirmed when the curator asked HEAD – Genève to participate in the exhibition with a new specific installation. It is this experience that the practice-based approach of the seminar has expressed its full potential. The *Stoned in the Bathroom* installation, presented here in essay form, is inspired by a laboratory product of the bachelor of interior architecture course during the Spring semester of 2019, entirely dedicated to the theoretical and scientific issues raised by the "Intimacy Exposed" seminar. It confirms not only the value of the approach but also the fertility of a research field that is only just beginning.

The buildings, environments, and artistic expressions presented in this volume highlight the rich past of domestic technology and the ambiguous future of personal and collective practices in the dense ream of toilets. Partial and fragmentary tales of an ideal, semantic, physical space about which much remains to be told. From this perspective, this book presents a beginning. Its authors are aware that there are more absences than presences and there are many issues which, within the permitted time and space limits, it has not been possible to cover. One of them is our interest in the production of more precise, appropriate and far-sighted knowledge in the design of sanitary facilities and "wet areas". We must bear in mind that social problems linked to public and private health are largely yet to be addressed in developing countries, i.e., precisely where these issues are most pressing and many projects are underway. The exploration of past and contemporary habits in the use of sanitary spaces and body care is limited to a very few cases that can only shed limited light on the galaxies of

interiors, furniture, objects, and constructions provided by toilets, bathrooms and restrooms. Our hope is that this volume, and all that is not in it, provides inspiration for readers to study these galaxies and draw new stimulating, *bathiful* constellations in them.

MODERN PLUMBING
Alexandra Midal

"The bathroom is part of our brain, contributing to the unique growth of the individual mind."
                                                    —Richard Buckminster Fuller (9)

The two visuals chosen to communicate the symposium that brought us together, "Intimacy Exposed. Toilet, Bathroom, Restroom", raised questions. The call for projects was launched with a photograph showing two series of urinals placed on either side of a room with yellow walls and a black and white checkered floor. Instead of signifying the necessary diversity of toilets, the choice fell on the urinal, an symbolically male device, as if it were the synecdoche of the toilet and by extension, the bathroom. This presupposition betrays the masculine predominance that governs the production of spaces, and toilets as well.

Secondly, a photograph was circulated to announce the symposium, and what did it show? Two young women, students from the Interior Architecture Department, dressed in swimming costumes, facing the lens. As a preamble, I asked myself how and why these two students posed in this outfit for a photographer. And then I wondered about what this political and aesthetic choice was meant to state. Finally, I tried to understand what relationship this cliché had with the issue of intimacy and toilets.

Might it be the feminine counterpart to the previous image, showing two rows of five urinals? How might we analyze this scopophilic scene? A scene in which two young female students, backs to the wall, as in mugshots taken by the police, are reified. They look like objects of contemplation in a scene that highlights

9   Excerpt from the documentary *The World of Buckminster Fuller*, Directed by Robert Snyder, Baylis Glascock, USA, 1974, 85 minutes.

10   Laura Mulvey, "The Spectacle is Vulnerable: Miss World, 1970," in *Visual and Other Pleasures* (London: Palgrave Macmillan, 2009), 3–5.   11   In the domestic space, this split responds to the idea of the feminine as "angelic," praised by poets such as Coventry Patmore in *The Angel in the House* (London: John W. Parker and Sox, West Strand: 1854) and repeated in specialist work on the education of young women or "Angels in the house" as John Ruskin calls them, benevolent wives who must pool their efforts to create an emotionally and psychologically serene environment for their exhausted husbands. In England at the end of the 19th century, the founding fathers of design gave women a mission: to build a shelter to protect their husbands from the tribulations and evils to which the modern city subjected them.   12   In *Privacy and Publicity* (Cambridge: MIT Press, 1996), Beatriz Colomina combines these two mass media images of the bidet and the urinal, placing one above the other. See also: Beatriz Colomina and Mark Wigley, "Toilet Architecture: An Essay about the Most Psychosexually Charged Room in a Building," *Pin-Up Magazine* no. 23.   13   *Fountain* went from product to work of art with the addition of the signature "R. Mutt" on the front left, above the handwritten year "1917." The year did not

the contemporaneity of the thesis outlined in the seminal analysis by Laura Mulvey and Margarita Jimenez almost fifty years ago (10). Aren't we once again confronted with the concept of the "paradox of phallocentrism", sometimes subconscious, made famous by Mulvey in her seminal essay, "Visual Pleasure and Narrative Cinema"?

Clearly, by questioning the choices underlying the way "Intimacy Exposed. Toilet, Bathroom, Restroom" was communicated, our introduction may seem controversial, but that is not our intention. It aims to demonstrate, if need be, that the issue that brings us together today is political, and that it is essential for us to examine it. Choosing pictures of urinals and scantily clad young women raises questions about the prevalence of unchallenged masculinity and the decorative status in which women are circumscribed, regarded as the decorative elements of intimacy (11). With *Modern Plumbing*, our aim is to relate, through the narrow lens of plumbing, certain scattered events steeped in an ever-present form of androcentrism. This seems to refer to Marcel Duchamp's urinal which he bought in a shop, and the bidet that Le Corbusier took from an industrial sanitaryware catalog. (12) The architect chose a photograph of a violin-shaped bidet by Maison Pirsoul and published it in *L'Esprit Nouveau* in 1923–1924, six years after Duchamp sent *Fountain*, a white earthenware urinal produced by J. L. Mott Iron Works, to the Society of Independent Artists' exhibition in 1917 (13). Alongside the urinal that "furnishes the public domain" (14)

and collects urine, the bidet furnishes the home and cleans secretions. Urinals, bidets and toilets fall within the scope of "pipework" both literally and figuratively. They are part of the vast project of "domestic Taylorism" (15) driven by women proto-designers who worked towards the invention of a rational organization of the home, and the history of design and architecture.

The virtues of waste

Paulette Bernège, director of the Mon Chez Moi publishing house and President of the League for Household Effifficiency, tracked down examples of seemingly mundane work done by women in the domestic sphere such as "saboteur stairways", "'tiring' materials" and above all "vampire distances." These, however, suck up the energy spent by the housewives' untimely comings and goings: "I call these poorly studied distances that drain human forces 'vampires'." (16) In so doing, Bernège pleaded for a civilization of pipework that linked chimneys to the human body and radiators to waste water. She enveloped her statements with drawings interspersed through her essay entitled, *Si les femmes faisaient les maisons* (If Women Made Houses, 1928). Her way with words echoed the ones finely crafted by her model, American professor of household science and contributor to the *The Designer* magazine between 1920 and 1929, Christine Isobel Frederick. Bernège made

indicate the year of the urinal's production but rather, its deliberate artistic appropriation and display at an art event. It also owed this new status to Alfred Stieglitz's photography. Indeed, *Fountain* was not displayed at the American Society of Independent Artists: it was supposedly misplaced behind a partition for the duration of the event. It then met its destiny in the construction of its fantastically modern, mass-media legend thanks to Stieglitz's photograph, which was first published in *The Blind Man*, the avant-garde magazine co-edited by Duchamp, where it appeared in front of a plant signed with the photographer's name. For his part, Le Corbusier took the Picoul violin-shaped bidet and published it. The public discovered it in the pages of his magazine, *L'Esprit Nouveau*, then in the pages of *L'Art décoratif d'aujourd'hui* in 1925, where it served as an opening for the chapter entitled "Autres Icônes Les Musées". For Le Corbusier, its presence justified the condemnation of the arbitrariness that he accused museums of and dismissed in favor of "real" museums, which, he said, were exhaustive, brought together all the objects of life and erased all separation between art and everyday life.   14   Fanny Beaupré and Roger-Henri Guerrand, *Le Confident des dames. Le bidet du XVIIe au XXe siècle : histoire d'une intimité* (Paris: La Découverte, 1997), 124.   15   Paulette Bernège, *Si les femmes faisaient les maisons* (Paris: Mon Chez Moi, 1928).   16   Bernège, *Si les femmes*, 13.

her work known in France as early as 1915, and Frederick found her alter ego in Bernège, the European pioneer in the teaching of "modern scientific household management" (17) and the science of domesticity for women. The celebration of this domestic and scientific concept gained momentum and echoed a timid recognition of the importance of women in American society, (18) while it remained almost non-existent in Europe.

A theorist of domestic life, Frederick coined the concept of "creative loss", an economic notion according to which consumption, the driving force of the nation, must favor waste and loss. By following a transformation circuit similar to organic digestion, the economy reproduces the circulation of food ingested by the human body until it is excreted. With this notion, Frederick asserted the importance of the body. Initially published by the Butterick Publishing Company and in *The Ladies' Home Journal*, "creative loss" emerged as the capitalist and consumerist expression of the rational organization of the body and the household as applied to the economy and society. This notion was seen as a progressive act that developed, according to the late 1990s analysis by Ellen Lupton and Jack Abbott Miller in *The Bathroom, the Kitchen, and the Aesthetics of Waste: A Process of Elimination* (19) into an ethos of the disposable. The oxymoron "creative loss" highlighted the redeeming role and culture of waste, and propelled it into the highest spheres of morality. The importance of this analogy between body and society, in order to function well, was a focus on destruction which would ensure a kind of renewal. Above all, Lupton and Miller showed how rationalization was the product of the dual obsession of modern America, fascinated by the avalanche of new products and a

Figure 2.5. Illustration accompanying Allene Talmey, "A World We'll Never See," *Vogue* (1 Feb. 1939): 90. Constantin Aladjálov/*Vogue* © Condé Nast Publications Inc.

plethora of diets that promised to reshape your body to your liking. This is one reason why American consumers euphorically celebrated the principles of planned obsolescence, which served the idea of an economy engaged in a cycle where goods are continually ingested, digested and expelled, only to be absorbed again, all under the guise of an aesthetics of fluidity where the digestive system, nature and culture, home and the economy merge. A similar apology for fluidity was advocated by all the designers of the Streamline movement. This was the first modern American design movement, one of whose most important figures, Norman Bel Geddes, illustrated its benefits in his designs, as in *Magic Motorways* (1940), (20) a book that looked at the country's highways.

Eugenics in the bathroom

To illustrate their hypothesis, Lupton and Miller focused on the importance of modern plumbing in circulating city water and wastewater, and the mobility of toilets and pots, the original portable objects that gradually became fixed (21) and spatialized in the household. This ground-level installation gave rise to the functionalization of a place then assigned to ablutions and body care. From objects, these items of furniture became industrial enameled porcelain equipment for the modern bathroom. Their

17   Christine Frederick, *Selling Mrs. Consumer* (New York: Business Bourse, 1939), 284–285.   18   For more about this question, see Alexandra Midal, *Design by Accident, For a New History of Design* (Berlin: Sternberg Press, 2019).   19   Ellen Lupton, J. Abbott Miller. *The Bathroom, The Kitchen, and the Aesthetics of Waste* (New York: Princeton Architectural Press, 1996).   20   Norman Bel Geddes, *Magic Motorways* (New York: Ransom House, 1940).   21   Beaupré, *Le Confident*, 135.

22   Le Corbusier evokes the need to create a "Law of Ripolin", to ensure that all interiors are painted white to target any form of dirt or darkness. *L'Art decoratif d'aujourd'hui* (Paris: Editions Crès, 1925), 192. Ripolin is the brand name of the hard impermeable and washable enamel "sanitary paint" invented at the end of the nineteenth century, promoted for its anti-bacterial properties, and favored by hospitals.   23   Christina Cogdell, *Eugenic Design: Streamlining America in the 1930s* (Philadelphia: University of Pennsylvania Press, 2004).   24   In 1939, Geddes was not the only industrial designer to promote eugenics, the body and design. *Vogue* magazine invited eight all-male industrial designers, Russel Wright, Walter Dorwin Teague, Donald Deskey, Raymond Loewy, Henry Dreyfuss, Egmont Arens, Joseph B. Platt and George Sakier, to design the garment for the "Woman of the Future" as part of its special issue devoted to the New York International Exhibition, whose theme, *The World of Tomorrow*, explored future scenarios. The Loewy-designed dress appeared on the magazine cover, worn by a woman whose body in profile was facing the future. Although focused primarily

easily washable white surface was meant to reflect the simple, pure and hygienic white order and other Laws of Ripolin that appeared at the turn of the 20th century. (22) As Cristina Cogdell pointed out in *Eugenic Design* (23), the intertwining of Bel Geddes and eugenics forged an association where excess flirted with an ideology that merged with Streamline and also found defenders in Henry Dreyfuss and Raymond Loewy, who claimed its moral expression and hoped to select objects as well as bodies, thus transforming them according to their aerodynamic industrial design with pure, streamlined lines in order to save society. Reflecting their functionalist obsession, the Streamline designers thought they were working to improve the human race. Moving in this way from the body to comfort to the organization of the household demonstrated the disruptions that sometimes accompanied the rise of progress and its ideological objectives, which were often nauseating in terms of scientific performance. (24)

As this concept spread to the interior and to the bathroom, constituting both its paradigm and its demonstration, the Modern movement established a regime of cleanliness that was meant to reflect the ideal of fluidity of continuous production applied in assembly lines in factories. For Lupton and Miller again, these standards of personal and household hygiene, from the kitchen to the bathroom, accompanied health and hygienic reforms and exceeded the requirements of architectural rationalism: "The

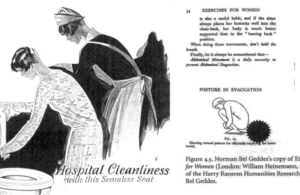

Figure 4.5. Norman Bel Geddes's copy of Ettie A. Hornibrook's *Restoration Exercises for Women* (London: William Heinemann, 1932), 54–55. In NBG Papers. Courtesy of the Harry Ransom Humanities Research Center and the Estate of Edith Lutyens Bel Geddes.

functional 'need' for clean bodies and clean houses has fed the culture of consumption, by mapping out the human and architectural body as a marketplace for an endlessly regenerating inventory of products". (25) Addressing the popularity of the discourse on the virtue of the body's fluidity, Cogdell illustrated her point with a reproduction of X-ray photographs showing the breakfast itinerary according to John Harvey Kellogg in 1918. She also presented a 1937 advertisement for Petrolagar laxatives extolling the benefits of an ideal intestinal transit where excrement, much like in a train arriving at the station at the exact time, circulated according to a precise timetable, in a punctuality amplified by a sketched hand holding a stopwatch at the bottom left of the advertisement. She analyzed programmatic drawings such as *Postures in Evacuation; Exercises for Women* from Hornibrook's book (26) in Bel Geddes' library. These drawings recommended and indicated the correct posture to adopt for defecation. Only women were depicted, as if they were the only ones who could relieve themselves of the risks of "abdominal stagnation", while men were not concerned with these issues, busy as they were designing that selfsame toilet. This was the case of Henry Dreyfuss,

on her clothes and accessories, the Streamline designers did not hesitate to comment on the physique of the woman of the future, predicting a perfect body and mind, according to their bias in favor of masculine symbols, through the application of triumphant eugenics applied to everything and everyone. See Christina Cogdell, "Products or Bodies? Streamline Design and Eugenics as Applied Biology," *Design Issues* 19, no. 1, 2003, 36–53, translated into French in Alexandra Midal, *Design, l'anthologie* (Geneva: HEAD – Genève, 2013): "For example, Deskey proclaimed, 'Medicine will have given her a perfect body. She will never experience obesity, skinniness, head colds, excess hair or a bad complexion thanks to a proven diet and a controlled basal metabolic rate. Her size will be increased and her eyelashes lengthened, with a little hormone X'. Because of her beautiful body, she will no longer need to wear underwear, he thought, and after a period of nudism, she will likely dress in semi-transparent fabrics, similar to togas. Teague's idea revealed that he also believed that most women would have 'beautiful bodies and that the current trend towards nudity would continue apace'. Sakier, for his part, said that, 'The woman of the future will be tall, thin and beautiful; *she will be brought up for that*, for the pleasure of the community and her own happiness… Her point of view will be clear and direct. She will be free of all kinds of complexes and inhibitions'."   25   Lupton, *The Bathroom*, 9.   26   Ettie A. Hornibrook, *Restoration Exercises for Women* (London: William Heinemann, 1932), 54–55.

for example, who imagined the *Criterion Closet* in the thirties: a low, violin-shaped toilet designed for Crane Co. Its unorthodox design was supposed to facilitate expulsion by relying on the springs of primitivism, according to which, modernity has distanced us from calls of nature. The itinerary of food responded to a healthy colon, its fluid transportation, that jewel in the crown of the automotive civilization and the liberal American economy. The latter was seen from an ergonomic and aerodynamic perspective as a territory to be colonized: "The consumerist body ingests and expels not only food—the prototypical object of consumption—but the full range of images and objects that pass through the cycle of manufacture, purchase and disposal. In this *process of elimination*, the body itself is remade." (27) And of course, such an allegory of good digestion focused on the richness of production and loss, between ingestion and excretion, and the economy, design and health referred to the toilet and the pleasure of the anal stage: "[…] 20th century design gradually articulated the bathroom and kitchen as the erotogenic zones of the domestic body." (28) Lupton and Miller's analysis also oscillated in the same proportions between desire, loss and sexualization: "As sexual pleasure is sustained by the utilitarian processes of digestion, the restless desire for new commodities built on fetishized routines consolidates biological consumption". (29)

Confident and confessor

Aside from their notoriously industrial character, the interest shown by Le Corbusier and Duchamp in sanitary facilities revealed the importance of the new "white order" of the 1930s, and a relationship with bodily waste that had become a subject in itself and could sometimes even be elevated to the status of a work of art. The bidet, however, belonged as much to hygienic and medical conveniences as it did to libertinism and lust. After having been straddled equally by men and women, its use changed after the demise of the old regime in France. The urinal and the *vespasienne* reserved for male urination were considered to be an instrument of popular and urban hygiene which "furnished the public domain", while the bidet, associated with cleanliness, was gradually considered to be an effeminate device whose use would be exclusively feminine.

The first mention of the bidet, according to the analysis of Fanny Beaupré and Roger-Henri Guerrand (30), reminds us how difficult it is to determine its etymological origin with certainty. It "[…] could potentially come from 'baudet'" (31) in one of these distorted linguistic mysteries that made it into a toilet object under Louis XIV back in 1739. It appeared on the calling card of master turner Rémy Pèverie, a cabinetmaker who offered "bidets with back and flap" and "double bidets that can be used by two people at the same time". (32) Beaupré and Guerrand noticed an amusing piece of information: the editor of the *Almanach des honnêtes femmes* reportedly proposed a

27 Lupton, *The Bathroom*, 9.   28 Lupton, *The Bathroom*, 8.   29 Lupton, *The Bathroom*, 8.   30 Beaupré, *Le Confident*.   31 Beaupré, *Le Confident*, 15 sq.   32 Beaupré, *Le Confident*, 36.

33 Sylvain Maréchal, *L'Almanach des honnêtes femmes pour l'année* 1790 (Bruxelles: de l'Imprinerie de la Société Joyeuse, ca. 1870), 11, mentioned in Beaupré, *Le Confident*, 20.   34 In this context, it might be a valuable circumvolution to note that Koolhaas's *Delirious New York* is steeped in sexual symbolism that runs through his 1995 opus *S, M, L, XL,* with delightful collaboration by Bruce Mau. The photographs cleverly echo the body of

"Fête du bidet" on 2 February, Candlemas Day, stressing the importance of the object and the intimacy that ladies shared with it: "Many ladies call their bidet their confessor. It erases all sins with perfect ablution". (33) The bidet played the role of confidant. Erotic literature was not to be outdone and took it in its stride. This was the case with Antoine Bret, *Le ***** Histoire bavarde* (Londres: 1749), where Urgande's young lover Cyparide is metamorphosed into a bidet and his male organ takes the shape of a sponge, thus associating onanism with the use of the bidet. It was perhaps in this same dynamic that Duchamp, father of the *Bachelor Machine*, wrote a cruelly funny note about Le Corbusier: "L.C.: case of early male menopause sublimated into mental coitus". Sublimation here referred to a geographical shift in creation where the architect and the artist defined the origin of modernity in a relationship between man and his body, while blending bodily functions and eroticism and constantly questioning the nature of this itinerary.

Washbasin Woman and Skyscraper Man

Surrounded by A. Stewart Walker as the Fuller Building, Leonard Schultze as the New Waldoorf Astoria, Ely J. Kahn as the Squibb Building, William Van Allen as the Chrysler Building, Ralph Walker as One Wall Street, D. E. Waid as the Metropolitan Tower and J.

H. Freedlandler as the Museum of the City of New York, Edna Cowan, also known as "The Basin Girl", was the only woman in the men's parade at the famous 1931 *Architects' Ball*. She walked around New York's dizzying skyline wearing a washbasin and double taps instead of the cigarettes and cigars usually offered for sale by young women in this type of get-up. In the guise of a new hygienic standard, alone among the dominant architects, Cowan wore a plumbing system and exhibited a reproductive rather than a creative loss. In *Delirious New York*, his "retroactive manifesto" as he calls it, an indictment of Le Corbusier's decongestion, Rem Koolhaas chose to display these two photographs of the *Architects' Ball*: in the first picture, a row of delighted men dressed in their respective New York skyscrapers, naturally erected vertically; and in the second, Edna Cowan carrying her basin on her belly as if it were a symbolic extension of her organs. Her solitary presence in a masculine architectural universe speaks of the isolation of women and the hierarchy that prevailed in architecture. (34) To better understand the sad banality of this situation, we must bear in mind that after completing E-1027 (1926–1927) in Roquebrune, Eileen Gray spent many months there with Jean Badovici. Around 1938–1939, Badovici invited Le Corbusier to stay there, but when he left, the modernist masterpiece was found vandalised.

the text, and certain exchanges operate as mysterious clues left here and there to be deciphered by the reader, responding to each other in distant chapters within the book's 1345 pages. Such is the case with the first image representing the Villa Dall'Ava, the first private construction built by Koolhaas. The photograph shows a large white geometric area in the centre of the page. The represented volume is surrounded by the greenery of the future site. In making this choice, Koolhaas postulates, as did Le Corbusier previously, that before anything is built, a site contains architecture waiting to be revealed. The second clue to this rebus can be found in another chapter "Strategy of the Void". The first image is a black and white photograph of a naked woman more or less side-on, in which she grasps a geometric shape with her hand, represented by a black bar. We can tell from the state of the sheets that this is a sex scene, and that the lady is grabbing a penis. The volume corresponds to the shape of the Villa Dall'Ava. Both images are constructed in the same way: the black volume echoes the white, turning these forms (a work of architecture and a penis) into an area of correspondence or even interchangeability. With Koolhaas, the erectile metaphor of skyscrapers is replaced by a geometric area and reproduces the established hierarchy. The comparison via this camouflage of two initially identical forms serves on the one hand to embody the creative force of the male architect and on the other, refers to the reification of the woman whose creative role is, at best, reproduction.

Naked, as the photographs show, the guest painted the fresco *Sous les Pilotis* on one of the walls of the house. With phallocratic impunity, he had committed an offence that disfigured Gray's architecture. Emblematic of the sexual politics at stake, Le Corbusier's act was a clear attack on women and their architecture and production.

Strategy of the Void

Duchamp was not to be outdone, if we believe his possible misprision with *Fountain*. Recently discovered documents about the work of Baroness Elsa von Freytag-Loringhoven query the attribution of this major work in the history of modern art. In a letter dated 11 April 1917 by Marcel Duchamp to his sister a few days before the exhibition, he mentioned that one of his friends, under a male patronymic, sent *Fountain* to the New York exhibition. It seems that the name "Richard Mutt" might have been the pseudonym chosen by von Freytag-Loringhoven, who lived in Philadelphia at the same time as Duchamp, and that she might have been the author of the work, not Duchamp. If she did not take offence at this, unlike Gray, who ceased all contact with Le Corbusier, this may have been because the work was rejected, and because she died ten years later, in 1927. Duchamp would then have let people attribute the authorship of the work to him in 1935, without batting an eyelid. Another sculpture by von Freytag-Loringhoven entitled *God* (c.1917) is explicitly a masculine mirror of *Fountain*. Von Freytag-Loringhoven exposes this *God* made of pipes, and one can understand the

reasons why the father of the *Bachelor Machines* appropriated this work, which so successfully questioned the symbolism of plumbing and addressed a pseudo-transaction and circulation between the feminine and the masculine. One cannot help but notice the extent to which these sexual manipulations partly explain the eradication of women in the history of design and architecture by modernists such as Nicholas Pevsner *Pioneers of the Modern Movement* (London: Faber & Faber, 1936) published in 1936 or Reyner Banham *The Architecture of the Well-Tempered Environment* (London: Architectural Press, 1969), his work on air conditioning, networks and plumbing, where no woman, not even in a swimming costume, is ever studied.

Toilets are very special places
Michael Jakob

Shortly before one of the most famous sequences in film history, in Alfred Hitchcock's *Psycho*, Janet Leigh, alias Marion Crane, writes "I regret stealing $40,000" on a piece of paper and throws her scribbles into the toilet. As Crane strives to wash both her body (one remembers the shower scene) and her conscience clean, we witness the first time a throne is flushed in film history. We see and also hear it.

In French, one may say of certain things that they appear "*déplacé,*" not where they should be. The epiphany of the throne in *Psycho* was of course interpreted as such a displacement. Toilets were censored in film, and it was inappropriate to show this sort of thing in movies. By "displacement," my intention is not to refer to mathematics, physics, or politics, but rather to play with the sense of place while reflecting on toilets. Toilets are generally situated in places where the user can both feel displaced (in a strange place) or, on the contrary, in their place (in a safe, intimate place). To depict or to speak about toilets or about what we do in toilets is generally a displacement: one

should not speak about such places. Architects and artists have played with this sense of displacement by placing toilets (or elements linked to them) where they normally should not be, or by simply highlighting them.

In a famous aphorism, Viennese critic Karl Kraus stated:

"Adolf Loos and I, he literally, and I, grammatically, have done nothing more than to show that there is a difference between an urn and a chamber-pot and that culture plays on this difference. The others however, the defenders of positive values, can be divided into two groups: those who use the urn as a chamber-pot and those who mistake a chamber-pot for an urn." (35)

The difference stated by Kraus between the two poles, urn and chamber-pot, at the heart of "culture," is, however, by no means absolute. The distinction between them or better, the system for which the chamber-pot is a symbol, is full of objects that are permanently *displaced*, and here lies my main argument. The toilet or bathroom and its specific objects are, in other words, an experimental ground for continuous displacements. The difference between the urn and the chamber-pot is not absolute, because they share a certain *Unheimlichkeit*. They are both uncanny, the chamber-pot because of its liquid or solid content and the urn for the precious substance it contains, our ashes. "Culture" or civilization consists of displacing (hiding) systematically, at least from the englightenment onwards,

35   "Adolf Loos und ich, er wörtlich, ich sprachlich, haben nichts weiter getan als gezeigt, daß zwischen einer Urne und einem Nachttopf ein Unterschied ist und daß in diesem Unterschied erst die Kultur Spielraum hat. Die andern aber, die Positiven, teilen sich in solche, die die Urne als Nachttopf, und die den Nachttopf als Urne gebrauchen." Karl Kraus, *Die Fackel*, No. 389/390, 1913, as quoted in Arts Council, *The Architecture of Adolf Loos* (London: Arts Council of Great Britain, 1985), 42

death (the ashes) from the city to secluded places (the modern cemetery), very much in the way modern hygienic theory and practice displaced *excrementa* and *urinae* from inside to a secure outside, i.e., to a state of invisibility. Civilization is—and here Kraus is quite right—synonymous with the fundamental distinction between the pure and the impure, theorized by René Girard, among others. (36) Civilized humans never ceased to remove "it", to put it out of sight and out of reach from our olfactory organs. The term used in different languages to name "it"—"ça" in French, "es" in German—is another expression of our desire to rid ourselves of something impure by placing it in a neutral context, where the importance of the human body and its implications are repressed. Architect Adolf Loos, quoted by Kraus, infamously installed a sink in the vestibule of his *Rufer house* (1922). The sink stands in "a sunken nymphaeum, where it gazes out from its alcove, oddly outside everyday operations and the spaces of the household." There is of course, "no towel or soap, [this is] a sink only to look at." (37) The sink is *not* in the toilet, but in the entrance hall of the house. It is therefore not only displaced itself, but also displaces the senses of the observer from touching (ambiguous) to seeing (from a safe distance). Loos generally liked to displace things in order to complicate and complexify his interior designs. At first, this rather unusual sink seems to allude to holy water, a kind of sacramental protection at the threshold of the house. The suggested purification is, however, completely unnecessary in this kind of space because here, the perpetually clean sink is part of a clean house. What it does, as a supplement—in

36   René Girard, *La Violence et le sacré* (Paris, Grasset, 1972).
37   Daniel S. Friedman, Nadir Lahiji, *Plumbing: Sounding Modern Architecture* (New York, Princeton Architectural Press, 1997), 39.

displacing us—is to create a sense of aesthetic impurity: the strange object disturbs the purity of the construction. There is another famous example that could be added to our catalog of displaced elements linked to the restroom or bathroom. This time, we are in Le Corbusier's *Villa Savoie*, in Poissy, near Paris. Here again, the sink is placed where it should not be, in the entrance hall. In the manner of a readymade object, the white sink reminds us of the qualities of modern living: purity, functionality, and freedom from useless elements. This practice of what Siegfried Giedion calls "befreites Wohnen" (free living) is, however, expressed by a fundamentally useless and bizarre object, the sink, moved from the bathrooms of the house to the entrance. As a symbol, the useless displaced sink reminds us of the advantages of victorious civilization, the history that brought us (humankind) from the microscope to the observation of germs and bacteria to Pasteur and pasteurization, to vaccines, fresh water, modern sewage systems, and so on. Le Corbusier himself had a complicated relation with his body. He loved to be photographed naked, in a nudist pose (sunbathing), he died by drowning, and according to François Chaslin, he was never really interested in sexuality. (38) That an artist should revert the habits of daily life by displacing the device used to clean oneself and thus making it highly and unusually visible is not really a novelty. For instance, as Jean-Claude Lebensztejn has shown, (39) peeing men are a frequent *topos* in European art. Even the absolute purity of sacred personae has

38   François Chaslin, *Un Corbusier* (Paris, Seuil, 2015).   39   Jean-Claude *Lebensztejn*, *Figures pissantes: 1280–2014* (Paris: Macula, 2016).

been juxtaposed against the mundane 'problems' of humans who have to pee or defecate in order to live on. And what to say about François Rabelais (a writer with genius and a physician), who invented an entire encyclopedia of things that the human body has to expel:

"Then he [Gargantua] dunged, pissed, spewed, belched, cracked, yawned, spitted, coughed, yexed, sneezed and snotted himself like an archdeacon, and, to suppress the dew and bad air, went to breakfast, having some good fried tripes, fair rashers on the coals, excellent gammons of bacon, store of fine minced meat, and a great deal of sippet brewis, made up of the fat of the beef-pot, laid upon bread, cheese, and chopped parsley strewed together." (40)

For Rabelais, whose famous *torch-cul* or ass-torch episode is equally famous, the human body is a source of a profound wisdom linked to the otherwise forgotten practices of a 'lower' order (in contrast to, for instance, the purity of the mind), a hidden treasure later analyzed by Sigmund Freud, among others. For Freud, the things contained in the bowels of a child can be expelled or retained. A child can 'punish' his parents by not going to the toilet or he can do it, his inner contents thus becoming his first "gift".

Under the regime of modernity, it is in any case essential to isolate "it" by isolating the person freed from "it". One has to isolate and protect both the single individuals and the group from "it", to remove "it" from sight and smell. Modern purification practices (in Thomas More's *Utopia*, the chamber-pot is be made of gold) become possible thanks

40   "Puis fiantoit, pissoyt, rendoyt sa gorge, rottoit, pettoyt, baisloyt, crachoyt, toussoyt, sangloutoyt, esternuoit et se morvoyt en archidiacre, et desjeunoyt pour abatre la rouzée et maulvais aer: belles tripes frites, belles charbonnades, beaulx jambons, belles cabirotades et forces soupes de prime." François Rabelais, *Five books of the lives, heroic deeds and sayings of Gargantua and his son Pantagruel,* trans. Peter Anthony Motteux and Sir Thomas Urquhart of Cromarty (London: Lawrence and Bullen, 1892), 112.

to *spatial* strategies, i.e., the construction of specific *loci* in which to liberate ourselves: toilets, restrooms, bathrooms, water-closets. Since the 19th century, we have learned to use these very special "rooms of our own". The *toilet* (I shall use this general term) belongs first of all to a *system*. Its main qualities (each of them a domain to be explored) are:

a.   The idea of safety and protection, the possibility to do "it" (and of course other things) and to wash oneself inside a closed space, sometimes even closed with a key. An important consequence of this situation is a new sense of (bodily) intimacy. But how does intimacy actually work? Is it not a process, submitted to cultural influences rather than something given?

b.   The inside/outside relationship, because there is still a sense of permeability and circulation between the inner and the outer zone. Water penetrates these very special places, while "it" leaves the room, exactly analogous to the process of the human body. The toilet is therefore highly anthropomorphic. The toilet as a cell is part of a larger organism, which consists of the totality of toilets linked to a nearby hydrological system (water supply), a sewage system, the regeneration of water, and so on. The toilet is a place of transition, of translation, and at the same time, of control and order. Before modernity, everyone could do "it" wherever they wanted, while now (since roughly 200 years ago) people are assigned to a specific place where they have to do it and clean their body. The system can be enlarged and take the form of Urinopolis, the important 19th century Parisian project aimed at collecting the urinae of the Parisians and transforming it into fertilizer.

c. The toilet (cf. a) as an isolated place does not normally have windows. But instead of windows (a view outside) it has mirrors. The scopic regime of the toilet is that of introspection, of reflexivity. Modern and postmodern introspection takes place less in the confessional (where one is not alone) than in toilets. I see myself, I observe myself. But this seeing is actually a "cleansing" as well, a cleansing of the soul. Such a general statement requires further specification. In 1975 in Italy, for instance, a law was passed to make both windows and bidets mandatory elements, which can be quite a surprise for foreign visitors to Italy. A foreigner in Italy feels displaced, while an Italian in France can feel the same because of the lack of bidets. (The quite pathological version of the toilet mirror complex is the one we encounter in the *Shining*.)

d. The toilet, considered as a private place, contains (besides the sink and the loo) an inner world, a veritable realm of toilet objects: soaps, combs, creams, cologne, shampoo, etc. In 17th century France, Louis XIV was already the sole and exceptional user of a toilet room of his own (while all others used shared locations), where he camouflaged his smell with perfume.

e. The toilet is differentiated and often gendered, for example by the bidet. It can be racially differentiated too, by discriminating between people.

In short, looking back at the 20th century, we can see that the toilet became increasingly clean, cold, and almost hospital-like. This corresponds to a form of civilization characterized by the cleaning instinct (*Putztrieb*), the wish to stay "clean" and "pure." In Veneto, they use the saying: "*Fai puíto*", "Stay clean." And why do people say "*stronzo*" or "*Scheisskerl*" all the time, and call the other "a piece of shit"? Is it a way to keep the other away, the person who could infect us with miasma? Our use of such formulas transfers the uncleanliness to the other, *he* does "it", while *we* control "it". The other (always a potential enemy, according to Sartre in *L'être et le néant*) is a priori "a piece of shit", "*une merde*", "*una mierda*".

20th century toilet or restroom architecture reinforces this tendency by transforming the peehouse and shithouse into a temple of purity, pure form and cool design. Because of this relation with the other, the toilet is at the same time totally solipsistic (individualistic) and totally collective (linked to society and its control over us as subjects, *subjectum*).

Here again, the logic of displacement is at work: the postmodern bathroom is even cleaner than the modern one; it is clinical, cold, cool; it tries everything to avoid looking like a bathroom, and its being-a-bathroom is hidden by a superficial stratum of beauty. "*Ceci n'est pas une toilette*" (*ou salle de bains*) could be the secret slogan of such places, while they are, of course, still, *des toilettes*.

The person who understood all such aspects of the processes linked to the circulation of liquids and the modernistic rituals of purification was, naturally, Marcel Duchamp. His infamous *Fontaine* is a masterpiece of what I call displacement. Duchamp took an industrially-manufactured porcelain urinal, which he signed as "R. Mutt", and proposed it to the Society of Independent Artists in New York for their 1917 exhibition. Taken out of its context, i.e., displaced, the urinal was intended to be displayed at the exhibition, but for reasons that are not completely clear, it was displaced and placed behind a curtain. The meaning or the identity of the readymade is marked by displacement as well: the urinal became the *fountain*. A fountain is normally a place where people drink, where water comes out, appears, while the urinal is the place where the liquid comes in, disappears. By creating a urinal-fountain or a fountain-urinal, Duchamp provoked a shock that was probably the motivation for the conservative reaction to hide an object not fit to be displayed in the center of an art exhibition. The mystery of this almost mythical piece of art is further complicated by the fact that it was photographed in Alfred Stieglitz's studio, and that a version of that photograph was published in the Dada journal with the significant title, *The Blind Man*.

The disappearance of Duchamp's *Fountain* can be interpreted in different ways. It can be taken as a symbol of what we want a urinal to do: to make everything related to our bodily existence that we do not want to retain disappear. In becoming placeless, lost, the Duchampian readymade does exactly what the system intends to do: to create a

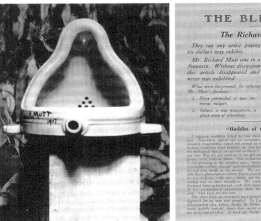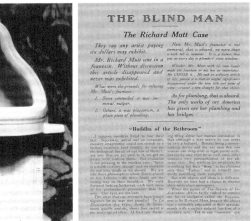

clean slate or *tabula rasa*, total cleanness. Furthermore, the artist signed his work with a pseudonym, "R. Mutt." In "Mutt" we can read, besides the transposition of J-L. Mott Iron Works in New York (where he most probably purchased the object, manufactured in Trenton, New Jersey), "Mutter," the mother, the matrix. The urinal-fountain is a place of origin, linked to the sphere of liquids where we humans originate. But what about the origin of this piece of art? Part of its legend is linked to the anonymity of the artist who was to present it. Several individuals were linked to its *mise-en-scène*. Was the origin of this work of art as such *displaced* by Duchamp, who claimed that it was his, while in fact it belonged to more than one artist? "Mutt" also reminds us of "*muet*", i.e., "mute", and "mutt" is also a name given to bastard dogs (quite fitting for a "bastard" work). The signature *on Fountain* cannot be fully identified. The handwriting looks like Duchamp's, but equally it could belong to the person who sent it from Philadelphia to New York. The name Richard Mutt changes continuously with the context, just like the object it is connected to, that changed location prior to its disappearance, only to reappear again in Duchamp's later works. Thanks to its scandalous existence and epiphany, this work of art created an awareness of the things that happen "normally" when we deal with objects related to the toilet as an instrument for removing things.

There is yet another work of art connected to Duchamp, the mysterious Baroness Freytag-Löringhoven, a third artist, Morton Livingston Schamberg, and moreover, to the toilet/bathroom/restroom complex. It is called *God*, and it is a cast-iron drainpipe. With the urinal and the drain trap, the world of the plumber entered the world of art, bringing to mind Duchamp's remark, "The only works of art that America has given are her plumbing and her bridges". (41) The over-designed toilets and contemporary temples of purity should thus be interpreted as what they are: places with a dark side as well, places intended to hide something. Total purity and the perfectly designed, flawless body remove something. They *displace*, letting us know that they are doing so. The permanent displacements linked to the realm of the toilet remind us that toilets do not want to be what they are, i.e., toilets. Instead, they want to be temples of the clean and the pure, atmospheric places undisturbed by miasma of any kind or by any outside intruder. The toilet, which is not a toilet while still being a toilet, corresponds to a subject with a body without disturbing elements on which it depends. Not a body that is peeing or shitting. Hypermodernity celebrates the bodyless body, the engineered persona we encounter in universes such as *Westworld*.

Luckily, art has another story to tell by shocking and surprising us. Art displaces our certainties and asks us not to forget "those things". Kubrick's *Shining*, Pasolini's *Salò*, Manzoni's *Merda d'artista* and many other artworks invite us to explore the unknown territory of bathrooms, restrooms, toilets. Too much purity brings us back to the existence of impurity.

41   Marcel Duchamp, *The Blind Man*, (New York : H. P. Roché, May 1917).

42   Stephen Calloway, "Edward James' Interiors," in *A Surreal Life: Edward James* (London: The Royal Pavilion, Libraries & Museums, Brighton and Hove, Philip Wilson Publishers, 1998), 94.   43   The exhibition *The Thirties: British Art and Design after the War* ran from October 25, 1979 until January 13, 1980 at the Hayward Gallery on London's Southbank.

In 1932, British artist Paul Nash designed a bathroom for the Austrian dancer and film star Tilly Losch. The bathroom was commissioned by poet and surrealist art collector Edward James for his London home at 35 Wimpole Street, where he lived with the feted Losch during their short and tempestuous marriage. Although made for a private house and unlikely to have been seen or experienced by many, the bathroom captured the public imagination and garnered critical acclaim at the time of completion. Art historian Stephen Calloway, whose essay in a monograph on Edward James is the most extensive account of the surrealist patron's visionary approach to interior design, writes,

> "The one truly extraordinary room in the house [35 Wimpole Street], Tilly Losch's glass bathroom, was not one that was generally seen; however, both from a small number of photographs published at the time and perhaps even more by word of mouth, it gained a considerable degree of celebrity and came to be considered as undoubtedly one of the key interiors of the decade." (42)

Tilly Losch's glass bathroom was Nash's only completed work of interior design, and was damaged in London bombing during World War II. Surviving pieces of the interior were removed from Wimpole Street in around 1947 and taken to James' family home in West Dean, Sussex. The excavated parts remained there until the bathroom once again became an object of fascination and exemplar of progressive modern design from the 1930s when it was presented at an exhibition at the Hayward gallery in 1979 on art and design of the period. (43) It entered the V&A collection shortly afterwards.

Nash's original decorative design achieved the integrated harmony of light, space and colour he believed essential for modern habitation. The room—the modern realm of the apartment or bedsit as opposed to the entire house as inhabited by earlier generations—"is of importance and must be considered seriously", he wrote in *Room and Book*, (44) a collection of essays published in 1932, in which Nash set out his view on modern design, architecture, book-making and the challenges of professional practice. In a chapter entitled "The Room Equipped," Nash writes:

"'We live in a conscious age… and the dearest wish of most people today is to be aware, first of themselves and then of their surroundings.'… 'So what time there is must be spent in self-expression,' and one means of 'expression' is found in 'creating' what is called 'our own surroundings'". (45)

Nash's bathroom design is of significant interest as an example of his pursuit—through his painting and design work—of structural harmony and variety through surface, pattern and composition to create, "a world to inhabit in which one might enjoy the forgotten luxury of contemplation". (46) Testing his architectural ideas in practice would not have been possible had it not been for Edward James' own voracious commitment to creating such unique surroundings for himself in his inherited properties in London and Sussex and, after the war, at his sprawling ranch in Xilitla, Mexico.

The Nash/Losch bathroom was reconstructed for the Hayward exhibition by the same company that had originally installed the bathroom at Wimpole Street, and entered the V&A collection after it closed in early 1980. The

44 Paul Nash, *Room and Book* (London: Soncino Press, 1932) 45 Paul Nash, "The Room Equipped," in *Room and Book*, 33. 46 Nash, The Room Equipped, 54.

acquisition of the Losch bathroom was subject to much internal discussion at the V&A, because the interior consisted of a mixture of original, period, and remade fittings. According to a file note on the object's provenance and acquisition, Roy Strong, director of the V&A at the time, regarded it as "phoney". Nevertheless, the V&A pursued and agreed to the acquisition, and the bathroom has remained in the collection until the present day. It has never been reassembled for display at the V&A, and there are very few photographs of the original and its faithful reproduction. (47) Despite this lack of documentation, I was as captivated by these photographic records as the design interested readership seeing and reading about this stunning modern bathroom and "total" work of art when first published in the 1930s. The invitation to speak at "Intimacy Exposed" coincided with my own research into complete rooms and significant interior and architectural fragments in the V&A collection, which could be returned to public display—or indeed displayed for the first time—at V&A East, a new satellite project due to open in the Queen Elizabeth Olympic Park in London in 2024. The context of the research for this paper is our attempt to define which of the V&A's many interior architecture treasures can and should be displayed at V&A East. Paul Nash's bathroom for Edward James and Tilly Losch is a significant example of the conceptual unity of art, design, and interior architecture, and a fascinating story of the importance—and drama—of artistic patronage in the early 20th century. That the site of this highpoint of creative expression is the seemingly humble domestic bathroom makes this object even more intriguing.

47 Photographic, press, and curatorial documents are held in object record files at the V&A. A few photographs of the re-made bathroom are available through the RIBA image website (RIBA Pix, https://www.architecture.com/image-library/) and images in the Hayward Gallery archives.

48   Peter B. Flint, "Tilly Losch, Exotic Dancer, Is Dead," *New York Times*, December 25, 1975, https://www.nytimes.com/1975/12/25/archives/tilly-losch-exotic-dancer-is-dead.html, accessed September 1, 2019.

49   For a detailed overview of the intersection between Nash's works of art and design, see Inge Fraser, "From A Sheet of Paper to the Sky. Pattern in the work of Paul Nash," in *Paul Nash* (London: Tate Publishing, 2016).

Ottilie Ethel Leopoldine Herbert, Countess of Carnarvon (1903–1975), known professionally as Tilly Losch, was an Austrian dancer, choreographer, and actress trained in classical ballet and modern dance. She worked across Europe and the USA, performing in both theater and film, and also worked as a choreographer. Losch's *New York Times* obituary recalled the "exotic dancer" acclaimed by critics for her "superb grace," "brilliant technique" and "much personal charm". (48) She was noted for the fluent use of only her hands and arms, which spun a captivating, rhythmic imagery. Edward James (1907–1984) was born to a wealthy industrialist and a socialite. The family had aristocratic connections and his godfather, King Edward VII, was rumored to have been his father. James was an Eton and Oxford-educated poet, art collector, and patron of enormous independent resources who embraced surrealism and amassed one of the world's most significant private collections of surrealist art. He moved in avant-garde literary and artistic circles, and his properties in the south of England and London became the center of his most celebrated collaborations and commissions. James first saw Losch perform in 1928 at her London debut of Noël Coward's musical revue, *This Year of Grace*. James was twenty-one and Losch twenty-five. The young aesthete was instantly entranced and quickly became obsessed with the beguiling dancer. Their relationship was tempestuous and short-lived, causing a scandal when they divorced in 1934 after three years of marriage. James accused the notoriously cruel Losch of having an affair and she counter-sued claiming he was homosexual, although James was in fact bisexual. Losch lost the appeal.

Paul Nash (1889–1946) was a British artist most well-known for his surrealist paintings and art produced in the context of the two world wars as an official war artist. He was revered for his multidisciplinary practice, which included book-making, textile and product design, photography, illustration, set and interior design. He embraced an integrated approach to art that ranged from the surreal to the decorative and applied arts. Nash's work painted during and after the Great War were a literal and metaphorical exploration of the devastating physical and psychological effects of war. As his surrealist visual language developed, Nash's work interwove the haunted landscapes of the mind with British coastal scenery where the effects of war scarred the terrain. He employed recurrent illusionistic devices such as the mirror and the frame, which gave his deeply personal landscape subjects a domestic and architectural quality. Like many leading modern artists of his generation, Nash designed posters for corporate clients including London Transport and Shell, and extended his formal language of disrupted perspectival space and surreal, abstracted representation to the world of advertising and communication design. His work with British manufacturers included designs for glassware, textiles, books, and patterned paper. Nash lamented the parochial, sentimental idea of the 'fine arts' and urged that the field of the artist should encompass applied art and that patterns should be considered as important as paintings. (49) His interest in shifting perspective and pattern was used to dazzling effect in his bathroom for 35 Wimpole Street.

Edward James was familiar with Nash and his work, but the only documentation found in the Nash Archive at Tate, which describes their relationship at the time of the bathroom commission, was a note from Nash to his wife stating that, "James has bought *Swan*—bless him". (50) This pithy insight suggests a friendly personal relationship between artist and patron.

For James, art was life. He expressed his passions and inner world through surreal and extravagant interior design. James' marriage to Losch inspired an extensive remodeling of 35 Wimpole Street that catalyzed a lifelong commitment to the "realization of fantasies through decoration" (51) in his domestic spheres. Stephen Calloway has compared James' behavior to that of a bowerbird, known for building and ornamenting its nest with shiny, colorful found objects.

Before exploring the unique collaboration between Nash, James and Losch, it is important to understand the context of James' artistic vision for his homes. Nash's 'Bathroom for a Dancer' was one of many intriguing interior and architectural projects that enabled James' surrealist interests to flourish in built form. James made minor renovations to his inherited family estate at West Dean, which included the smaller Monkton House designed by Edwin Lutyens in 1902. By 1935 Monkton had become James' passion project for a total surrealist artwork. Architects Christopher Nicholson and Hugh Casson, through consultation with Lutyens' son Robert, carried out significant renovations to the exterior as well as modernization of the interior. Bamboo drainpipes, palm-tree columns, illusionistic decorative plaster *trompe l'oeil* swags around the

50 Paul Nash to Margaret Nash, *Postcard,* May 20, 1932, TGA 8313/1/1/223, Paul Nash Archive, Tate Britain. 51 Calloway, "Edward James' Interiors", 98.

windows, a lilac exterior render and a roof clock showing the days of the week were playfully surreal interventions that made Lutyens' original design almost unrecognizable. James' close and creatively productive relationship with Salvador Dali came to the fore inside the house. In the 1930s, James was Dali's most important patron and they collaborated on a number of surreal objects such as the *Lobster Telephone* (1936) and the now iconic *Mae West Lips Sofa* (1937/38). Two of the sofas furnished Monkton House and the V&A recently acquired one example for its collection. When showing signs of wear and tear, Dali and James decided that repairs to the worn fabric were to be made into a decorative feature: appliquéd caterpillars crawl along the upper lip, adding a surreal, uncanny quality to the oversized lips. Richly patterned wall coverings and sumptuous furnishings completed the whimsical and fantastical experience at Monkton.

Throughout the 1930s, James commissioned a series of interventions and alterations at 35 Wimpole Street. The first significant alterations were bathrooms for himself and Losch. Geoffrey Houghton-Brown, a notable young painter known for his painted interiors and murals in a jazz-modern style, designed the new bathroom. The study for the modernistic 'Pompeian' mural in James' bathroom, now in the V&A collection, shows a washed decorative scheme depicting mythological scenes and illusionistic architectural forms. Nash's design is, by contrast, a triumph of modern materials and abstract composition. A committed Modernist, his use of industrial materials and glass "offered the most extensive realm of possibilities in modern architecture". (52) Again, in *Room and Book*, he

52 Nash*, The Room Equipped*, 51.

53   Nash, *The Room Equipped*, 51.   54   Nash, *The Room Equipped*, 51.

INTIMACY EXPOSED   A Bathroom for a Dancer   Catherine Ince

55   Calloway, "Edward James' Interiors", 94.

noted that, "its influence begins to change the character of interior structure and decoration. No other material contains so many elements of magic." He went on, "[…] a careful study of its application must stimulate the least imaginative mind and excite it to adventure". (53)

The Nash/Losch bathroom is made up of panes of colored and mirrored glass. Some were plain and others patterned with a mottled and dimpled surface texture, a feature designed so that the effect of steam and condensation on the glass did not destroy the overall interior effect. The glass panels were in shades of black, purple, and pink, which created a luxurious setting that was also dynamic, emphasizing Nash's bespoke concept for his dancer client. The irregular arrangement of the glass panels creates fractured reflections and a broken decorative rhythm to produce an ever-changing balletic mural enhanced by the room's lush and shifting color palette. "We are no longer interested in renovations. We are beginning to work in terms of architectural relations […] we are studying surface and grain, texture and vibration," (54) writes Nash.

Spatial and design elements such as the arabesque curves of the lighting fixtures, angled mirrored panels, and the bathroom's unique practice ladder underline Nash's choreography of the space and the disorientating sense of movement in his design. Photographers Dell and Wainwright adopted a New Objectivity approach to composition in their images for a period publication, capturing the dizzying sensation of experiencing the space through angled reflections. Imagining the body viewed in this space, Nash's use of mirror panels suggests a surrealist preoccupation with the body as explored in photography, particularly the intensely scrutinized female form and its often distorted, dismembered, and fragmented representation. There are no photographs of the bathroom in use, and indeed it is not clear if the practice ladder was ever used by Losch. The object is an appropriate playful motif in the overall scheme, and signals Nash's recurrent exploration of movement and three-dimensional pictorial space, in his paintings and illustrations from that time, using ladders and open-frame architectural structures. While little is known about Losch's involvement in the commission, Nash's environment is undeniably a performative space, a total artwork conceived for a dancer and choreographer. According to influential *Vogue* journalist Madge Garland, writing at the time, it was the *ne plus ultra* in bathrooms. (55)

In 1930, Nash submitted a design for an apartment interior to a competition run by the *Architectural Review* magazine. The fictitious client was "Lord Benbow", a Clydesdale shipbuilder, who was characterized as a traditionalist with an interest in sport. Nash's design for a "sporty" apartment is an exuberant, tongue-in-cheek rendering of the furniture of sporting activity—from football nets and rugby goalposts to tennis court markings and a bowling-alley like bar—transposed to the modern interior. The palette of materials prefigures the Losch bathroom. Here we see black and transparent glass, chromed metal, and the recurring structural forms and lattice patterns, which appear in his paintings, illustrations and textile designs.

Lord Benbow's apartment is a theater of fantasy and the Losch bathroom design is likewise a stage set, albeit one in which the intimate toilette ritual is performed alone or at most—we imagine—to an audience of one. The splendor and sensuousness of the interior suggests that other performances await, and Nash's design achieves the quality of an installation: a stage set with support structures and props for the protagonists of 35 Wimpole Street. The overlap of life and art was taken to further extremes when James commissioned Green and Abbot to produce a carpet leading to the bathroom bearing a repeat pattern of Losch's wet footprint. The carpet was redesigned for West Dean but, following their divorce, Losch's footprint was replaced with the paw-print of James' pet dog.

In 1933, in desperation to save his ailing marriage, James financed Les Ballets, a newly formed dance company enabling productions starring Losch to be staged in Paris and London. Sets for productions such as the ballet *L'Errante*, choreographed by George Balanchine with set designs by Pavel Tchelitchew, are reminiscent of the extravagant drapery of James' study at Wimpole Street. The surreal splendor of the interiors and decorative set-pieces such as the study and bathrooms, intensify the stage set quality of the house. The bathroom is both the site of an intimate, ritual performance and the backdrop to a performed life. The interiors and James' collection of props from original artworks to decorative and architectural objects take on the quality of a carefully staged installation: a 'total' architecture for an art-directed life.

The photo documentation of the re-staged bathroom at the Hayward Gallery exhibition in 1979 reveals the performative and glamorous nightclub-like quality of the space through Nash's use of architectural glass, lighting

and chromed fittings. The bathroom transforms from private to public space, awaiting activation by a cast of unknown but imaginable actors. For a major Paul Nash retrospective at Tate Britain in 2016, the cultural historian Michael Bracewell discussed Nash's work with exhibition curator Inga Fraser and artist Marc Camille Chaimowicz for *Tate, Etc.* magazine. Exploring the lineage of 20th century artistic practice and the blurring of boundaries between creative disciplines, Bracewell posits that it takes little for the viewer to "shift perspective and intention to view an interior like that as an installation." (56) He goes on:

"The uptake of ideas from the Modern Movement, Art Deco and the early 1970s by pop stylists was this notion that you took something from the world of fine art and you put it on the front line of mainstream pop culture, and you lived it […] But it is also on the aesthetic frequency of being in a very cool room, or a set for people in which to act something out. What interests me is the blurring between something that has been designed as part of the service industry and something which is being used as almost a prop."

Edward James' approach to interiors is perhaps the ultimate idea of an art-directed lifestyle. The uninhabited Nash/Losch bathroom awaits live theatrical or cinematic direction and speaks of a film-set as much as a stage or nightclub set. Promotional photography of the bathroom recalls a suite of photographs in the V&A collection by British photographer Bridget Smith. Taken in 1999, *Glamour Studio* documents the empty sets constructed for glamour photography in the pornographic industry. Smith writes, "I have chosen to photograph sets from the world of glamour

56   Michael Bracewell et al., "From the Surreal to the Decorative," Tate Britain, https://www.tate.org.uk/tate-etc/issue-38-autumn-2016/surreal-decorative, accessed February 4, 2021.

57   Scherf, Jone Elissa, Making *Your Dreams Come True: Young British Photography* (Ostfildern-Ruit: Hatje Cantz; 2001), 87.

photography, as play-acting seems such an integral part of dreaming. Each set offers the potential of the viewer to enter a new role and act out their own fantasies". (57) Here we see the collapse of private and public fantasy, the domestic and cinematic. Both bathrooms are poised, awaiting activity and human interaction to enable us to make sense of them. The mundane bathroom becomes a loaded space, inviting performance and transgression.

Paul Nash's bathroom for Tilly Losch is a rich and complex object. It exemplifies the pursuit of the total environment, a progressive expression of modern architectural and interior design ideas at play in the 1930s. It represents the exchange between art and design practice at the height of the surreal movement. Surviving photographic documents attest to the inventive dynamism and playfulness of this unique environment. It is a stage set waiting for the body in space to describe and bring to life its essential surrealist character. As with all 'restaged' interiors exhumed from their original context, what becomes essential is not just an engagement with the historical importance of the design of this object from behind the 'fourth wall,' but an encounter with its immersive spatial and physical experience. One must inhabit the room to truly understand its significance and design value.

POPULAR HYGIENE
(nothing fancy)
Marianna Siracusa

"The toilet is the fundamental zone of interaction between humans and architecture. Today we can imagine buildings without almost any of the other elements of architecture, but not without the toilet."   —Rem Koolhaas (58)

From an architectural perspective, the history of toilets in domestic spaces is not as long as one might think. A hundred years ago, most homes did not have an indoor toilet: it was usually located in an outside shed, a privy in the backyard. Although its outward appearance could be disguised, it was usually a bare, wood-paneled structure. The interior was invariably unglamorous. These facilities usually had a small window and were sometimes fitted with more than one seat. In order to allow air circulation, this room was not entirely sealed off from the exterior. Its main feature, however, was that it was not linked to the sewage system: the loo itself was simply a bucket that had to be emptied regularly. Between 1935 and 1936, photographers Carl Mydans, Frances Benjamin Johnston, and Walker Evans pictured backyard privies and rows of identical houses and outhouses across urban, suburban, and rural America as part of the Historic American Buildings Survey. The dimensions of these small identical facilities were all roughly one square meter or less.

58 Boom et al., *Elements of Architecture* (Cologne: Taschen, 2018)

Across the Atlantic in Italy, sanitary conditions in comparable dwellings were not so different. A good example is the plan of a *"casa a ballatoio"* or *"casa di ringhiera"* (the *ballatoio* or *ringhiera* being the gallery that provides access to each apartment), a type of popular housing built at the beginning of the 20th century. The typical plan had eight apartments per floor and the gallery always faced the back of the building, like the toilets. Every apartment had two rooms: a bedroom and a family room, and each room had a window. The family room would have a cooking area and a hearth. These 20 square meter apartments did not have indoor toilets. Instead they would share two latrines and two washbasins along the gallery.

In 1945, Federico Patellani documented the living conditions of Milanese *"case del formaggio"* (cheese houses). Between 1970 and 1973, for his project "Milano. Quartieri popolari," Gabriele Basilico also photographed the same typology of building in Milan's working-class suburbs, and these images show that shared outdoor toilets were still a reality.

Architecturally and socially, a lot has changed in order to arrive at the white free-standing bathtubs commonly advertised in contemporary magazines or the talking, music-playing toilets with integrated bidet, common in Japan, where they are known as "washlets". But at that time, only 40 years ago, the hygienic conditions of facilities in both rural and urban areas had evolved little. There has been a progressive move away from outdoor latrines. The flush toilet was invented in the late 16th century in England by Sir John Harington, but his innovation was ignored until the late 1850s when the so-called "Great Stink"

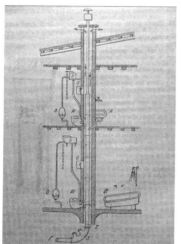

caused by London's untreated sewage forced the British government to start the construction of a new system of sewers for the capital city and to decree that every new house should have a water closet.

Back in Italy, architect and engineer Archimede Sacchi stated in *Le abitazioni* (1886) that latrines were a necessity: they should be well-lit, well-ventilated, and north-facing, to prevent the temperature of the small room from rising excessively. They should also be secluded and placed somewhere in the courtyard so that the entrance would not be visible from the street or the windows facing the courtyard. As a result, they were usually placed in a corner, vertically aligned around a central waste pipe or gathered in a small tower isolated from the main building. The "closet" was often very small, just large enough for a seat and its user. In time, toilets were connected to the sewage system, then later brought inside individual houses, but even then, the toilet was positioned on the margin of the dwelling, never directly linked to other rooms and never visible from the facade.

By the beginning of the 20th century, construction manuals were pushing for the toilet to be placed indoors. In order for the toilet to migrate inside, both the floor plan of the house and the design of the actual toilet seat had to change. The floor plan slowly allowed for the bathroom to be placed closer to the living room and bedroom. The object was made from a different material: instead of rough cast iron, it was in smooth

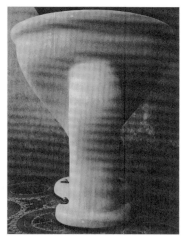

ceramic. It's easier for humans to accept the aesthetically pleasing rather than the ugly. This idea is explicit in "Excusado" (Toilet), a 1925 project by the American photographer Edward Weston:

"For long I have considered photographing this useful and elegant accessory to modern hygienic life, but not until I actually contemplated its image on my ground glass did I realize the possibilities before me," Weston wrote in his *Daybooks*. "Here was every sensuous curve of the 'human form' but minus imperfections." Weston spent two weeks studying and photographing ordinary plumbing fixtures from different angles, depicting their form instead of their function.

By 1925, manuals such as *La casa nell'igiene sociale, con note estetico-igieniche sull'arredamento* (59) published by Istituto Editoriale Scientifico were claiming that the latrine environment was an essential addition to the home. Health regulations of some Italian cities still allowed the existence of shared latrines but, while financially convenient, they caused great discomfort to all the tenants. The hygienic conditions were deplorable because none of the families would take on the task of systematically cleaning the facilities, and there was also the danger of cross-infection from family to family. Even the most modest dwelling—two rooms—needed to have a toilet.

"The latrine must never open directly either onto the bedroom nor onto the family room, or the kitchen if such a room is present. Some builders have placed the door in the small entrance area facing the staircase; others have done better, arranging a dressing room in which the sink and the shower can also be placed. Both the

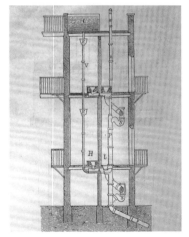

latrine and the dressing room must have a window. It would be advisable for the latrine closet to have additional ventilation, regardless of the window opening. The floor must be easily washable and even the walls must be made washable up to the height of a person—1.8 to 2 meters—and this can only be obtained by covering all surfaces with tiles".

Italian social housing apartments built in the 1920s covered 50 square meters on average: bedroom, 20 m²; family room, 15 m²; kitchenette, 6 m²; latrine, 1.5 m²; dressing room, 2 m²; entrance, closet and hallway, 5.5 m² per capita water consumption was 94 liters per day: drinking, 1.50 liters; cooking, 3.50 liters; personal hygiene, 22.50 liters; house and utensil cleaning, 13.50 liters; linen washing, 13.50 liters; latrine, 27 liters; various losses, 12.50 liters. An additional 48 liters had to be added for a weekly bath.

In a city like Milan, cesspools were still quite common in the 1950s, and could also be found in neighborhoods where there was a sewage system. It took some time for construction companies to comply with new regulations, but "hygiene" was eventually achieved: new indoor toilets were well-lit and ventilated rooms, with washable floor-to-ceiling tiles and fresh clean water. All residue was permanently eliminated, including odors. Out of site, out of mind, in theory at least. In fact, excrement does not disappear by magic. It takes a lot of resources—water and energy—to keep the unpleasant out of sight.

59   Ilvento Arcangelo, La casa nell'igiene sociale, con note estetico-igieniche sull'arredamento (Milan: 1925)

Once the toilet was accepted inside the domestic environment, further development was centered around form and the "liberal cultivation of the self", as the *Elements* catalog argues. Peter Greenaway, another Englishman, filmed *26 Bathrooms*, (60) a short documentary about that number of willing subjects using the most repressed room in the English home in the most imaginative ways.

For most of the 20th century, the priority for the toilet and the house in general was hygiene. In industrialized countries, this was generally—albeit not fully—achieved at the end of the 1970s and the beginning of the 1980s, accompanied by a great increase in the consumption of water and energy. Today, the average Italian consumes 250 liters of water a day. Common toilets use an average of 13 liters of water every time they flush, decreasing between 3 and 8 liters in efficient toilets.

But change never stops. The contrary is true. On the one hand, increasingly concerned about the environment, average dwellers are open to reconsider their everyday habits if this means reducing water and energy consumption. On the other hand, wellness has replaced hygiene in the context of domestic narratives, and this is pushing architects to do further research into the topic. We can expect the toilet to keep changing.

60 *Inside Rooms: 26 Bathrooms, London & Oxfordshire* (full title) is a short British documentary directed by Peter Greenaway and produced by Sophie Balhetchet in 1985.

FROM STUD TO STALLED!
Social Equity and Public Restrooms
Joel Sanders

This essay serves as a time capsule that captures one stage in the evolution of "Stalled!", an ongoing project that aims to create viable inclusive restrooms for everyone regardless of age, gender, race, religion or disability.

In both my teaching and practice, over the course of my career, I have been exploring the intersection of architecture and gender identity. The 20th anniversary of *STUD: Architectures of Masculinity* (61) has prompted me to reflect on the evolution of my thinking about gender and space. Strangely enough, this broader interest in the formation of gender identity and space has brought me back over and over again to consider an everyday space we take for granted: bathrooms. I am fascinated by bathrooms for a variety of reasons. Organized around water, bathrooms span multiple scales: they cater to the intimate needs of the flesh while relying on large-scale public infrastructures, plumbing, and sanitation systems to work. Encountered in every building type we design, they are among the most labor-intensive and expensive rooms to build. But what fascinates me most about bathrooms is that, contrary to the prevailing assumption that their design is determined by objective functional requirements, they are in fact places where a series of cultural, psychological, and technological forces converge.

Social and political context

At different moments in American history, the public bathroom has been a crucible that has registered social anxieties triggered by the threat of a series of marginalized groups entering mainstream society. Historical milestones include

61   Joel Sanders, *STUD: Architectures of Masculinity* (London: Routledge, 1996).

the introduction of the "ladies" room to accommodate women entering the workplace in the early 20th century, the fight to abolish segregated "colored" bathrooms by the Civil Rights Movement during the 1950s and 60s, the fear of contamination posed by gay men using public lavatories during the AIDS crisis in the 1980s, and the pressure to make bathrooms accessible to people with disabilities tied to the ratification of the Americans with Disabilities Act (ADA) in 1990. In each instance, the public restroom, by virtue of its being a physical space, transforms an abstract concern into a tangible peril, with the power to conjure nightmarish scenarios that compelled "normal" citizens to physically interact with "abnormal" people that society has preferred to render invisible.

In the United States, public restrooms are again a contested site, this time sparked by the specter of allowing a new constituency—transgender individuals—access to the public restroom belonging to the gender with which they identify. The moral panic over the presence of transgender people in sex-segregated public toilets is part of a long-simmering partisan reaction to overlapping cultural and political events. They include the Supreme Court approval of same-sex marriage in 2015, the 2016 Obama administration guidelines to Title IX clarifying that the federal law banning sex discrimination in education programs and activities also protects students who are transgender, and an unprecedented cultural visibility for trans people in mainstream media. This increased visibility and federal acceptance of trans people was met with considerable backlash. A high-profile example is North Carolina's

House Bill 2, which mandates that sex-segregated restrooms be used according to the sex designated on a person's birth certificate. More than two dozen similar bills attempting to restrict gender-appropriate public toilet access for transgender people have been introduced in State Houses across the United States, and the Trump administration has retreated from transgender-supportive interpretations of existing laws put forth by the Obama administration. Most recently, the Trump administration announced that they are rolling back the Obama-era Title IX guidelines, effectively erasing federal recognition of trans and non-binary people. As a result, battlegrounds will continue to be tangible architectural sites like restrooms.

Both sides of the debate claim safety as a central issue. Trans advocates cite high rates of violence faced by trans people in public restrooms, in particular trans women of color. Opponents claim transgender women pose a threat to cis-gender women, falsely portraying trans women as predatory men masquerading in dresses to stalk sexual prey in the ladies' room. Lurking beneath this unsubstantiated fear are long-standing societal anxieties about human embodiment and identity that bathrooms have historically harbored: they include abjection, misogyny, homophobia, heteronormativity, and ableism. However, a new and perhaps even deeper threat provoked by society's newfound awareness of transgender people is the destabilization of gender itself: trans people call into question the presumption that anatomy is destiny by demonstrating that there are multiple ways of expressing one's gender identity apart from one's biological sex that do not conform to the binary identity perpetuated by bathroom design through spatial segregation.

Stalled!

Stalled!, an interdisciplinary design research project spearheaded gender studies professor Susan Stryker, and law professor Terry Kogan and myself, aims to shift the terms of the debate in three fundamental ways. First, while all-gender restrooms have become a hot button issue that has received considerable media attention, few cover it from an architectural perspective. We need to regard public restrooms as a social justice issue with design consequences that can be solved with innovative architectural solutions. Second, we can no longer accept gender-segregated restrooms as a given that answers to the ostensibly objective needs of privacy based on anatomical difference. History teaches us that the first sex segregated bathrooms were instituted in the 1880s in response to women entering the workplace. A product of prurient Victorian values, "ladies rooms" were invented as havens for women who were presumed to be inherently fragile and ill-suited for the roughness of the male-dominated workplace. The ladies room was intended to provide women a home-like environment, a familiar domesticity while away at work. The space also served to protect women from men who regarded them as a temptation and distraction. And finally, we need to expand our purview to create inclusive restrooms that not only meet the needs of the trans community, but also encompass the needs of all embodied subjects of different ages, genders, and abilities.

There are two prevailing design approaches to gender neutral bathrooms: the single unit and multi-stall solutions. The single unit solution is the generally accepted code-compliant model that retains sex segregated bathrooms and supplements them with a single-occupancy room re-labeled/designated as Gender Neutral. However, this single-occupancy solution spatially isolates and excludes: it stigmatizes non-conforming individuals, not only trans people but also the disabled, by preventing them from mixing with other people.

Instead, we advocate a desegregated multi-stall solution which has received support from many trans activists. This alternative treats the public restroom as one single open space equipped with European-style, fully enclosed floor-to-ceiling doors that ensure visual privacy. This solution has numerous advantages. Gender non-conforming people will no longer have to choose between two binary spatial options that misalign with their identities. By consolidating a greater number of people in one rather than two rooms, there are more eyes to monitor the space, reducing risk of dangerous encounters. The multi-user type not only meets the needs of the trans community, but also a wide range of non-normative bodies traditionally neglected in public restrooms. Rather than focusing on gender alone, we are casting a wider net, developing inclusive guidelines that promote the mixing of a wide range of people of different ages, genders, religions, and disabilities.

Design methodology

Our goal is to enable the maximum number of differently embodied and identified people to interact in different settings while also providing options for those with unique functional or privacy needs. We recognize that there are ways of being different that don't allow for one-size-fits-all solutions: some people and communities have unique needs that require unique solutions. We have therefore developed a two-step inclusive design methodology represented in this diagram to foster sharing among individuals, families, friends, cohorts, and caregivers. First, we analyze the needs of a diverse list of end-users who perform specific activities related to the space, in this case restroom users, as they engaged in four activities: grooming, washing, caregiving, and eliminating. Second, we conduct a comparative analysis of overlapping end-user needs and activities from various constituencies. The outcome is a matrix of shared design strategies that guide material and finish choices, way-finding, lighting and the specification of furniture and fixtures.

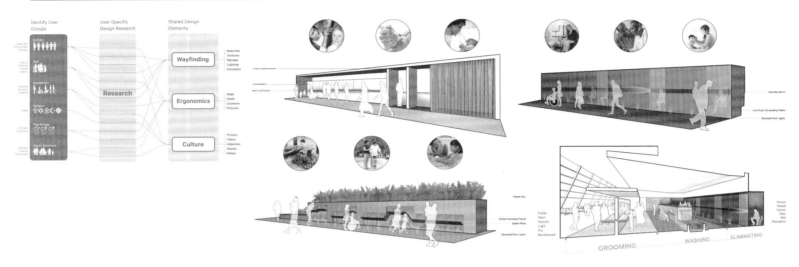

Gallaudet University prototype

Stalled! is in the process of developing two case study prototypes for inclusive public restrooms that attempt to take the multi-user solution a step further. The first is a collaboration with Gallaudet University in Washington DC, a school for the deaf that has been meeting the educational needs of "non-conforming" bodies since it was founded by Abraham Lincoln in 1864.

On the upper level of the Field House, we are working to retrofit typical sex segregated bathrooms into a multi-user facility, within the constraints imposed by the modest footprint of existing men's and women's rooms.

We begin by removing the existing plumbing stack wall and treating the bathroom as one open space. Then we remove the corridor wall and bathroom doors. Now the bathroom becomes a porous extension of the corridor. Next, we add two blocks of fully enclosed stalls in three sizes: standard, ambulatory, and ADA-compliant, as well as caregiving rooms equipped with a toilet, sink, and changing tables that allow for not only for caregiving between people of different genders, but also total privacy for those whose religions mandate sex segregation such as some Muslim and orthodox Jewish people. Then we add communal grooming and washing areas off the main circulation

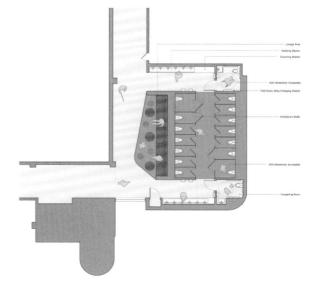

path. Finally, our scheme adds a lounge area that activates the corridor into an animated social space. The lounge is connected to a refurbished corridor activated by a series of alcoves for relaxing, working at laptops, or face-to-face conversations that facilitate deaf signing.

Airport prototype

Stalled! has also developed a prototype for high-traffic spaces like airports. We chose an airport as a case study because it is a high volume, mixed-use public space where a diverse constituency spends extended periods of time, catering to their mental and physical needs while they wait to board their flights.

Our scheme for the airport restroom takes the standard dimensions of a typical sex-segregated airport restroom as its point of departure. Our goal was to explore tactics that allow a wide range of differently embodied and identified subjects to perform a diverse range of activities; both the expected bathroom activities such as washing, grooming, and eliminating, as well as others such as administering medication, caring for children/infants, and performing religious rituals. Essentially, we aim to create a shared space that allows the maximum number of bodies to attend to their manifold needs while acknowledging that these activities have unique privacy and functional requirements.

Treating the toilet stall as a privacy unit allows us to remove the barrier that typically divides adjacent men's and women's rooms as well as the wall that separates them from the concourse, and instead, reconceive of the public restroom as a semi-open agora-like precinct that is animated by three parallel activity zones, each one dedicated to grooming, washing, and eliminating.

Slip-resistant sheets of diamond plate, tile, and rubber differentiate each of the three activity zones painted a different shade of blue for those with low-vision. After debating the merits of different color options, we finally chose blue because research indicates that it is soothing, associated with water, health and hygiene, and a complementary background color for deaf signing because it contrasts with skin tones.

Immediately adjacent to the concourse, the grooming station features a smart mirror that disseminates information (flight arrival and departure times, weather, and retail) while users groom at a multi-level counter that serves people of different heights and abilities. Those who want privacy can retreat into curtained alcoves for breastfeeding, administering medical procedures such as insulin injections, as well as meditation and prayer.

The communal washing station meets the needs of adults, children, people in wheelchairs, and people of short stature. Inset floor lights indicate the location of motion-activated faucets recessed into the wall that allow water to flow on inclined splash planes placed at different ergonomic heights. The water is then collected and cleaned in a remediating planter before being recycled. The scent of plants and the ambient sounds of flowing water masks bodily sounds and odors. Located at the back of the facility, the eliminating station consolidates rows of bathroom stalls that offer acoustic and visual privacy. Unoccupied stalls are indicated by recessed floor lights; when entered, they turn off and the now occupied stall glows from within. From the inside of each stall, users can surveil their surroundings by looking through a band of blue one-way mirrors at seated eye-level. The stalls contain low-flush composting toilets that treat human waste through aerobic decomposition.

As users circulate from one station to the next, passing from the outermost grooming station to the innermost toilet wall, they experience a multi-sensory gradient that takes them from public to private, open to closed, smooth to coarse, dry to wet, acoustically reverberant to sound absorptive, ambient to spot lighting.

Conclusion

Creating truly inclusive public restrooms is an ongoing project. Over the past hundred years, America has made some progress: milestones include the 1964 repeal of Jim Crow laws that mandated racially segregated public

bathrooms, and the implementation of the ADA in 1990, which required that public spaces, including restrooms, be physically accessible for people with mobility and sensory challenges. But there is still a long way to go if we hope to meet our goal of inclusive public restrooms that provide social justice, safety, and public health for everyone. The implementation of the bathroom typology we recommend, the multi-unit desegregated restroom, is not without challenges. First, it requires changes to legislation and building codes. This is why Stalled!, in partnership with the National Center for Transgender Equality and the AIA, lobbied the International Code Council to amend the International Plumbing Code (IPC), a model code that regulates the design and installation of plumbing systems in all types of buildings. Our efforts were successful, and the new version of the 2021 IPC will include a provision that allows for multi-user, all-gender restrooms.

Second, it requires changes to deeply ingrained social attitudes about the nature of the diverse bodies marked by gender, race, and dis/ability that use restrooms, and calls into question value judgments associated with practices that take place in restrooms. These values about embodied differences encoded in design standards and codes are not inevitable effects of biology and function, but instead historically contingent constructions that are shaped by changing social, psychological, technological, and ecological forces.

While important in their own right, bathrooms are a point of departure for a larger conversation about the relationship between environmental design, the human body, and social equity. The controversies surrounding transgender access to bathrooms is just one example of how the civil liberties of non-compliant bodies—women, Black people, religious minorities, immigrants, and the LGBTQ community—are imperiled in both the United States and the rest of the world by being denied equal access to public space. In short, these are political issues with architectural ramifications.

Architects and designers must accept their responsibility and explore the design consequences of these urgent social justice issues. Working in collaboration with activists, lawyers, code experts, engineers, and graphic designers, they need to form coalitions to develop a new design approach that enables a broad range of differently embodied people of various ages, genders, religions, and disabilities to productively interact with one another in public and private spaces. In the process of discovering creative design solutions that match the needs of diverse human bodies, we can change social awareness: accessible public spaces that foster mixing will breed tolerance and respect for human dignity and difference.

Since this talk was delivered in 2018, the Stalled! project has evolved and expanded its purview. Stalled!'s original impetus was social justice, a reaction to the culture wars surrounding trans bathroom access in the United States. While social equity remains central to the Stalled! mission, we have since learned from end-user and stakeholder feedback that restroom design is also a public health issue. In 2019, we began to collaborate on a research project with Yale Public Health, which found that the design of restrooms directly impacts physical and mental health. These findings prompted us to consider a wider range of end-users who perform an expanded repertoire of restroom activities, including people who menstruate, including trans men, people on the autism spectrum, people with shy bladder syndrome who fear urinating in public, and people who breastfeed. Stalled! 2.0 is a new prototype currently under development that considers these expanded end-users and activities along with the heightened hygienic standards for public space that we predict will be the aftermath of COVID-19.

And perhaps most importantly, Stalled! led to the founding of MIXdesign, an inclusive design think-tank and consultancy that is a branch of my architectural studio JSA. MIXdesign is dedicated to creating design recommendations and prototypes that meet the needs of traditionally marginalized individuals. We collaborate with institutional clients to make public spaces and everyday building types welcoming for people of different ages, genders, races, cultures, religions, and abilities. To learn more about the evolution of Stalled! and other MIXdesign initiatives, you can visit mixdesign.online.

GRADUAL INTIMACY
Philippe Rahm

To construct a building is actually to build a spatial pocket whose indoor climatic characteristics are more or less differentiated from those of the natural outdoor climate. The envelope (facade) of a building thus has two missions. The first is to filter out certain natural outdoor weather parameters that are considered uncomfortable, to keep them more or less intensely outside, to attenuate them, to cancel them out. Attenuate the temperature of the air that is too cold or too hot, attenuate the cooling wind, cancel out the rain, attenuate strong sunlight and its radiant heat, attenuate the humidity in the air. The intensity and direction of these filtration effects depend on geographical position, latitude, altitude, time of year and day, climate and weather variations. Then, conversely, there is an artificial intensification of certain climatic parameters in order to make the interior habitable, comfortable, breathable. The air temperature is increased in Canada in winter with a radiator, and lowered in Taiwan in summer with air conditioning. We reduce the air speed to warm up or increase it with ceiling fans in the tropics to cool down; we create light at night and more shade during the day. The building envelope thus plays a second role, that of containing the artificially produced climate inside by preventing it from mixing with that of the outside. And furthermore, it is necessary to thermally insulate air—and vapor-tight the inside from the outside in order to minimize heat loss in winter and heat gain from the outside in summer, to avoid the mixing of indoor and outdoor air, to minimize energy consumption and the energy necessary to create and maintain another (artificial) climate inside the building. This constructed indoor meteorology is daytime during the night, it is cool in summer, it is warm air in winter, it is less intense light under the burning rays of the tropical sun.

In places with a tropical climate like Taiwan, buildings are built to mitigate the excesses of the hot and humid climate to make it more habitable, more temperate, by lowering the air temperature to make it less hot, filtering solar radiation to make it less intense, less hot and less bright, to lower the humidity of the air and block out the rain. To modify the outside climate and make it comfortable inside, architecture works on two levels: the first level is the building envelope as a filtration of the outside climate, its attenuation. The second plane is the indoor climate as an artificial increase of the filtering effects. The climatic phenomena that are filtered and then conditioned indoors are mainly the heat of the air, its humidity, the radiation from the sun, the wind, the rain, and complementary missions such as the reduction of noise and sometimes air pollution.

Traditionally, architecture treats the first mission (the filtration of the excesses of the outdoor climate) by merging the filtration of the different parameters—those of heat, humidity, sun, rain, noise, and wind—in a single layer represented by the wall and the roof. This single layer used to combine all the filtration effects in a single response, in a single homogeneous line, in a single material, creating a clear and unique boundary between an uncomfortable, hot, humid, rainy, windy and noisy exterior and a temperate, dry, silent interior without rain or wind. This is historically explained by an ancient monolithic construction method that has since evolved a

lot. In the past, the wall was built in one piece using a single material such as stone, wood, or brick. And this single material alone managed and mixed all the tasks of filtering external climatic forces onto the interior of the building, creating a clear, unique boundary between an inherently uncomfortable exterior and a comfortable interior. Stone, for example, was equally the material that stopped the rain, blocked the wind, attenuated the outside temperature, reduced the amount of natural light, while also being the load-bearing material of the roof, which is simply the horizontal part of the filtering limit, in continuity with the walls. This unique type of separation between inside and outside no longer corresponds to the current reality of construction, which proceeds by means of the heterogeneous assembly of distinct layers of distinct materials, each one with a unique and specific filtration mission.

Cladding against burglary and physical shocks, air gaps between cleats for ventilation, watertightness, rainscreening, thermal insulation, working veils, support structure, airtightness, vapor barrier (vapor brake or vapor retarder), interior cladding, plaster, woodwork, paint, are thus the layers that we encounter when passing from the outside to the inside, each one made of a different material, precisely and specifically chosen or even invented by modern chemistry to match its objective of climatic filtration: to block water vapor, block water, block air and wind, block cold or heat, block light and to carry the slabs and the roof.

So today, there is no longer a single line, a single wall, a totalizing material that forms the boundary between inside and outside, and instead, a whole set of heterogeneous lines and materials which by habit are grouped together, arbitrarily juxtaposed, to form a simulated homogeneous wall, a block, apparently unique, unbreakable, indivisible, monolithic in appearance as a whole. In reality, however, today's wall is fragmented, segmented, a juxtaposition of different materials with distinct missions (watertightness, thermal insulation, screen, acoustic insulation, etc.), in addition to the application of dissimilar thicknesses, which ultimately form the wall.

When all the layers are kept together, we maximize the conditioned spaces, including some spaces that do not need to be conditioned, such as storage, technical or circulation spaces. We homogenize the climate of all interior spaces despite having access to detailed analyzes of the specific climatic objectives for each space. Today, if we want to limit energy consumption in buildings in the fight against global warming, then we must precisely and reasonably quantify the energy spent according to the type of premises, the type of activity that takes place there, the number of people who occupy it, the length of time they will stay there or only pass through it. The maximum comfort and energy must therefore be expended in interior spaces that will be occupied all day long such as offices, and minimum in spaces that are only occupied occasionally, such as corridors or staircases, or by non-humans such as warehouses, engine rooms or technical rooms. This means that in Taichung, offices should be very well insulated so that the heat from the outside does not penetrate the inside and the inside air can be artificially cooled to a temperature of about 71 ºF (22 °C) with the least possible loss of energy through

poor thermal insulation, cold bridges, cracks and airtight joints. As a result, the occupants of these rooms will live and work in comfortable climatic conditions. On the other hand, we can accept excessive heat in spaces that we just pass through, such as corridors, stairs, toilets or showers where we undress, because the occupants do not stay there for long and they can accept this punctual, momentary discomfort. By reducing the amount of air-conditioned spaces in a building, we proportionally reduce the amount of energy spent and the overall amount of greenhouse gases emitted, since even today, 91% of the energy consumed globally comes from carbon-based combustion.

What we are seeing in construction today is therefore this heterogeneous practice of dissociating what once was the homogeneous materiality of the wall into different layers, different materials and different thicknesses, based on the criteria of optimizing the effects of climate filtration. To combat the excess heat in subtropical environments for example, the building envelope will first filter the sun's rays, attenuate them, sieve them, and reduce their intensity or quantity in order to avoid radiant overheating of human bodies, skin, clothes, building materials, and furniture inside the building that are exposed to direct sunlight. This is the the sun blocker, low-emissive glazing, that interrupts the passage of infrared light from the outside to the inside, obviously an opposition of solid surfaces against the sun. This reduction of direct solar energy input by radiation will also reduce the air temperature inside by a few degrees. Next, we will distance the excessively hot outside air by thermally insulating the building with a continuous 20 cm thick layer of wool that traps billions of small air bubbles to prevent heat transfer by conduction from the outside air to the inside air that we want to keep cooler. Once the excess heat of the outdoor climate has been filtered out, the temperature of the indoor air is lowered by means of thermodynamic air conditioning.

To maintain the monolithic appearance of the wall, layers of dissimilar materials are usually grouped together on the same plane, which could equally well separate, space out, and expand from each other to form intermediate spaces with mixed climatic qualities in the way that the balcony, conservatory, pergola or bow window, for example, may have worked in the past. By expanding the layers that constitute the facade to create intermediate spaces between them, to make the in-between habitable, peeling the layers from each other, creating a habitable space between the watertightness and the thermal insulation, for example, the climatic richness of the interior spaces can be broadened, interior life can be diversified and the energy expenditure in the building can be reduced by only using air conditioning where it is really necessary.

The buildings that we have designed for the 67 hectare Taichung Central Park in Taiwan are a result of this dissociation of the usually single line of the building envelope into a multitude of layers, each one of which has a specific climatic property: for protection from rain, from heat, from wind, from noise, from intrusion or from sight. These different layers come together and diverge from each other to create habitable intermediate spaces, each one offering specific climatic qualities with its own mode of air conditioning, ventilation, and lighting.

Central Park is the urban attractor for a new 256 hectare district in the City of Taichung, Taiwan, built on the site of the old airport. The 67 hectare park has more than 10,000 trees and manages the rainfall runoff in the new urban district with retention basins that generate the park's topography. My team, Philippe Rahm architectes, in conjunction with Mosbach Paysagistes and Ricky Liu & Associates, won the international competition in 2011 and the park was officially completed and opened on December 6, 2020.

Taichung has a hot, humid, and polluted tropical climate. The ambition of the park is to offer cooler, drier, and less polluted places. The formal composition strategy of the masterplan is based on climate, cartography, and the design of the variations in heat, humidity and air pollution, which are superimposed to invent a multitude of microclimates and varied ambiances that generate aesthetic richness and a diversity of uses. The choice of location and species for the trees, the nature of the soils and the program are all guided by the climate. Thus, in places that are naturally coolest—due to their exposure to the cold north wind—we amplify the forest cover to create shade and thus double their freshness. The soils are rich in evaporative grass species with a high albedo to amplify the coolness. In locations farthest from sources of humidity, we amplify trees with floating roots to reduce their moisture content, and the soils are chosen for their particularly good drainage capacity. In areas far from roads, we increase the number of trees with hairy leaves to reduce air pollution. The program follows the climate: the less polluted areas are used for children's playgrounds, the drier areas are for sports, and the cooler areas are for various leisure programs.

The park is composed by its vegetation, but it also hosts some thirty buildings including a visitor center, the gardeners' building, two cafés, ten leisure follies, multi-use houses, and facilities buildings.

We have built nine public toilets amidst these facilities—small buildings scattered throughout the park. The construction of these toilets proceeds from a dissociation of the layers of protection and perception. Each one slides in relation to the other, from the outside to the inside, creating a concentric gradation of limits, from the most public to the most private, from the most exposed to the most intimate, from the most open to the most closed. The concrete area is defined first as the shaping of the ground, flat and passable, distinguishing itself from the natural environment of earth and grass. Further inside, a second area is formed by a set of loudspeakers that play music inspired by the sound frequencies of water noises, acoustically covering the noise of the toilet water. A third area is then built vertically from a grid that brings a little privacy to the common areas of the toilets. The fourth area is that of artificial light for the evening and night, composed of vertical luminous mats. The fifth area is the roof zone that provides shelter from the rain. The sixth area, where the toilets themselves are located, is the most private zone. It is shaped by a second screen that completely blocks views without obstructing the passage of air. Each of these layers has its own construction system, its own independent load-bearing structure.

The whole composition acquires the heterogeneity of the materials, lines, thicknesses, and dimensions, and composes a variety of spaces with as many climates. Each layer

slips in relation to the other, each architectural mission (walking on dry ground, being sheltered from view, seeing at night, being protected from rain, not being bothered by the noise of neighbors or one's own self) finds a specific, proper spatial incarnation.

UNDRESSING METHODOLOGIES
Louise Lemoine and Ila Bêka

Louise Lemoine: We were initially very surprised to receive an invitation to take part in this seminar. In fact, we had a good laugh thinking about being considered the experts on cleaning ladies, mops, and buckets since our first film, *Koolhaas HouseLife*. (62) But being invited to talk about toilets was definitively a new step!

Then, obviously, once we dived into the subject, above all its social history, we were amazed to see how polysemic and interesting the issue was. We really thought that we should have explored the WC world much earlier! The issue is so closely related to what we have been doing for more than 10 years, i.e., making films that question the standard values of architectural representation, transgressing many taboo issues. Our films were aiming to introduce a "crack of reality" in the very polite rules that govern the genre of architecture films. We wanted to observe buildings as they are in their pure nudity. But the WC was probably the last step that we never really took. WCs are so primordial to our domestic economy and at the same time so absent from the public debate that they would be the perfect subject for us! So, the time has come!

Instead of talking about toilets and bathrooms in history in a very objective kind of way, let's talk about a film about toilets that we haven't made yet. Challenged by the title of the seminar, "Intimacy Exposed", we thought it would be appropriate to expose

our own intimacy, not physically, by undressing—the surprise effect wouldn't last enough for the duration of the lecture—but rather by exposing the intimacy of our working methodology. The idea is to start a sort of a working session on the issue of toilets with the audience, exposing and explaining how we would build a film around the topic.

We will start by creating a sort of map of the subject in all the ramifications of its meanings. We will draw a constellation of words, drifting through the multiplicity and diversity of the meanings of this single word, *TOILET*, in order to expand its possible echoes. This is the way we usually start working on a subject, so we will share the process with you to give you an idea about the film we could potentially make.

So, let's start this game, as we may call it: let's draft a script for a film that doesn't exist yet. Now I am drawing the first point, which is *WC*. That stands for *TOILETS*, but it also encompasses restrooms and bathrooms in a larger sense. I'm using the word *WC* because its imagery is much stronger than the larger spaces for cleansing that it can include. From this single word, we can stretch out a wide variety of connections, a little bit like Gaston Bachelard's work on the poetics of the four elements. So, let's start with the first big star in this constellation. From *WC*, we will create connections to *BODY*, *WATER* and *EVACUATION*, which is the first of our euphemisms for evoking the system dealing with human waste.

62 Ila Bêka and Louise Lemoine, directors, *Koolhaas Houselife* (BêkaPartners, 2013).

Our first constellation puts four different elements, four different things, into tension: the physical reality—*BODY*—a natural element—*WATER*—a physical need—*EVACUATION*—and a space issue—*WC*—or the *toilet*. Put together, these four elements instantly create a sort of dynamic, close to fluid mechanics. Personally, we are always very interested in understanding the cultural associations, the psychological projections and the fantasies surrounding a specific space, and for sure, toilets have some of the deepest connotations.

Returning to our constellation, let's add to *WATER* all its "satellites", as we may call them. So, the first ramifications would be *CLEANNESS, CARE, HYGIENE* and *HEALTH*, which we locate here in the north-eastern section. Proceeding from here, a second ramification could be *WARMTH*, if we think of warm water, and thus the idea of *REST* and *COMFORT,* which leads us to *PROTECTION, REASSURANCE* and then *HEDONISM*. On the opposite side—because obviously it also works by contrast—you have: *VULNERABILITY*, then *ENCLOSURE, SECURITY*, and *SECRET*.

If we go back to our central dot BODY, as satellites in the first ring we will have: *NUDITY, PRIVACY*, and *PLEASURE*. Then, if we analyze the ramifications spreading out from *NUDITY*, it would be linked to *INTIMACY, GENITALS, SENSUALITY, EROTICISM, PLEASURE, DESIRE, SEXUALITY, INDECENCY, IMMORALITY, EXHIBITIONISM*, and *LUST*. Moving out from *PRIVACY*, a second ramification could be *DISCRETION, RESERVE, PRUDISHNESS, POLITENESS, GOOD MANNERS* and also *EMBARRASSMENT, SHAME, FEAR, MORALITY*, and *RELIGION*.

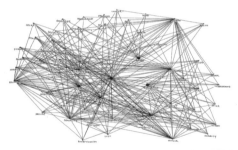

This is obviously non-exhaustive. It is a kind of initial constellation of ideas that we had (as the film does not exist yet). However, after listening to all the insightful lectures today, we could extend all these ramifications much further.

If we go to the 'star' of *EVACUATION* and we build its satellites, as a first ring we could have *EXCREMENT, DIRT* and *TABOO*. A second ramification, spreading from *EXCREMENT*, could lead to *WASTE, RELIEF, SEWER, UNDERGROUND* and *HIDDEN*. If we take *DIRT*, we could add *STINK, DISGUST, REALISM, ANIMALITY*. And if we take *TABOO,* that connects to *TRANSGRESSION* and *UNSPEAKABLE*. And then, I could add *BAD*—in opposition to good—and then *SCANDAL*. And obviously that leads us to HUMOR.

Drawing the secondary connections, it gets very complex graphically, but it is also very efficient in revealing intimate relationships between physicality, space, and morality, because the map itself expresses very clearly how Western culture has built its conception of the body on the Christian sense of guilt and the idea of original sin.

So, building up some secondary connections between the underlining themes and their satellites, it is very interesting, for instance, to take *EXCREMENT* as a starting dot. From here we could create a connection between *WASTE, UNDERGROUND* and *DISGUST* or we could connect it to *ANIMALITY, ENCLOSURE*, and *UNSPEAKABLE*.

On the other hand, if we take *HYGIENE*, we can build some secondary connections between *NUDITY, SECURITY,* and *FEAR*, or *DIRT, PRIVACY*, and *REALISM*. As you can see, each time we connect a physical notion to a spatial question and a moral value. If we take *PLEASURE*, for instance, it creates links between *GENITALS, TOILETS*, and *RELIGION*, which is pretty interesting. Or if we take *SEXUALITY*, we may create some connections between *EXCREMENT, SECRET* and *LUST*; or *HEALTH, SECURITY* and *TABOO*. Or if we take *RELIGION*, for instance, it creates connections with *PLEASURE, UNDERGROUND* and *IMMORALITY*; or *NUDITY, SECRET* and *SHAME*. Or let's take *HUMOR* as a starting point, which lets us make connections between *STINK, TOILETS* and *EMBARRASSMENT*, or we can have *GENITALS, SECRET* and *TRANSGRESSION*.

I could do a lot more, but I think you have got the idea. What we like is that you can clearly read that the various themes all include issues related to spatiality, physicality, moral values and emotions.

We can even see this drawing as a geographical map. In the north-east, we have what we could call the "body ecology" with *CLEANSING, HYGIENE, WATER,* etc. In the south-east, we have something more like the "animal body" with its needs and functions. In the north-west, we have the "social body" or what we could call "the ashamed body" (it sounds better in French: *"le corps honteux"*). Finally, in the south-west, we have the "released body", or the desiring body.

So, let's say that through this thematic constellation which we have built here together, you can get an overview of the working methodology we use each time we start wor-

king on a film, or a space. If we have to deal with a specific architecture, we use this sort of thematic mapping before we start to build up the film. The idea has been to share with you, almost live, how we could start thinking about a film on this subject.

Ila Bêka: I would like to stress just one thing: as we make films, what we have just seen is obviously only the preparatory work, an equivalent to a script, which is something that disappears as soon as the film appears. What is the script in cinema, anyway? It is a sort of list of things that you have to do in order to make the film. So, you have Scene One, Scene Two, Scene Three, etc. Every time we are invited to talk about our films, at the end of the presentation, a lot of people ask us, "Do you write a script? How do you prepare your films? How do you prepare what you are going to film?" It is then that we show this kind of scripts. I imagine you can't really build an idea of how the film will look from this. It is not very rational nor pedagogical. Let's say it's more a sketch of ideas resulting from earlier discussion that Louise and I have on the topic, on the polysemy of its meaning, and from which we elaborate these thematic connections and tensions. This happens before actually going to the place we have decided to film. For example, for *Barbicania*,

we made a very big script, before actually heading to the Barbican. How did it evolve then? We printed that big "graphic scenario", you might call it, and pinned it on the wall. It essentially serves as a thematic structure for us to guide the process of the film. We have worked in this way since our first film, *Koolhaas Housewife*. We draw this kind of fragmented script and at the end, the structure of the film very much resembles it. All our films are built as collections of fragments, little chapters that we call *fragments*. They are this way because this is the way we work: we don't have an order in mind when we start filming. We just find things. When we are filming, we are completely curious, attentive, looking for what is happening all around us. That's how we work.

For this particular conference, we have prepared this graphical script in a rather accelerated process. But since we have it now, we are ready to shoot the film! We only need to find the right place where we could make it. For more than 10 years now, we have worked—and are still working—on the architecture's body in a very organic and biological sense, so making a film about toilets makes complete sense!

I could say that my dream is to make a film in a very big tower, the tallest tower in the world, but only filming about how excrements are treated there: a film about the path of the excrements from the highest point down to the bottom… it would be fantastic! After we produce the script, there is also a second step that I need to mention: the one in which we create relations with other images we have in mind, images from other films, paintings, books or even sounds. So we just pass from the script to its

references, watching other films on the same topic, everything that might inspire us when we are making these kinds of films. We would like to list some extracts from four films that you probably all know, because they are very famous. All the same, they are still very interesting to revisit bearing in mind that we are dealing with the issue of toilets.

Blake Edwards, *The Party,* (1968)
Louis Buñuel, *Le fantôme de la liberté*, (1974)
Peter Greenaway, *Inside room: 26 Bathrooms, London & Oxfordshire*, (1985)
Danny Boyle, *Trainspotting*, (1996)

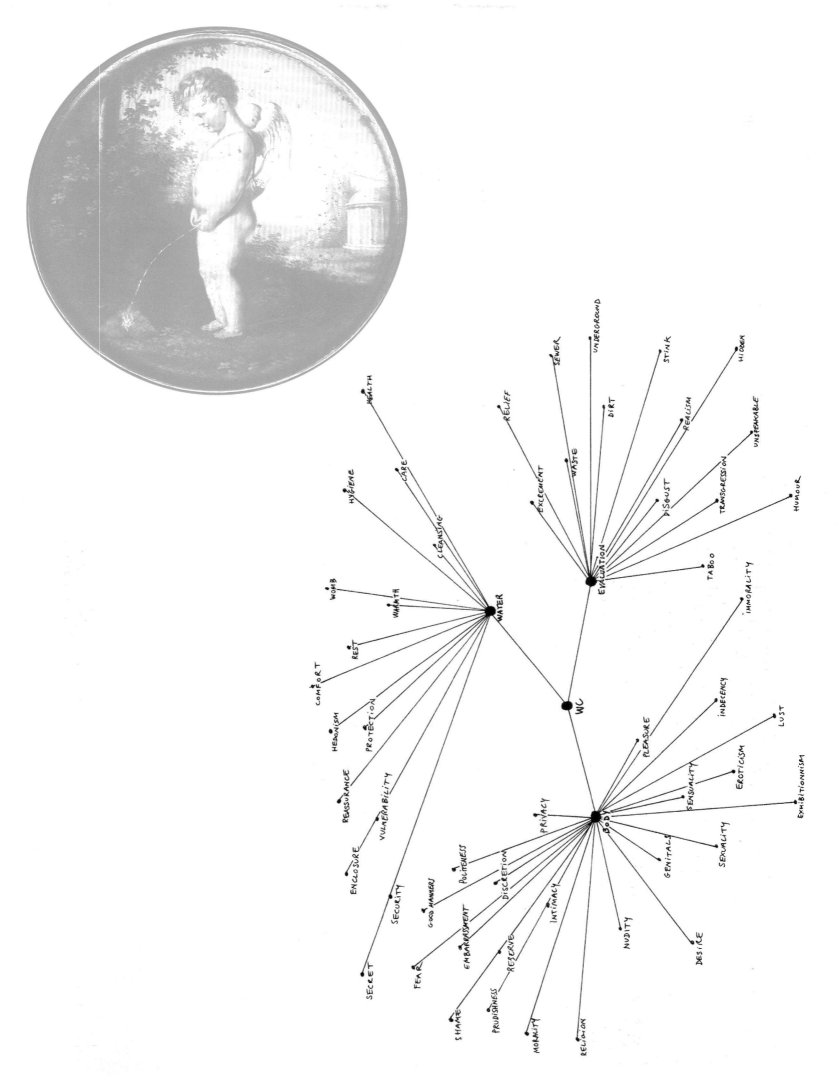

WATER
— HYGIENE
— HEALTH
— CARE
— CLEANSING
— WOMB
— WARMTH
— REST
— COMFORT
— HEDONISM
— PROTECTION
— REASSURANCE
— VULNERABILITY
— ENCLOSURE
— SECURITY

EVALUATION
— RELIEF
— SEWER
— UNDERGROUND
— DIRT
— STINK
— WASTE
— EXCREMENT
— REALISM
— HIDDEN
— DISGUST
— TRANSGRESSION
— UNSPEAKABLE
— HUMOUR
— TABOO
— IMMORALITY

WC

GOD
— PLEASURE
— INDECENCY
— SENSUALITY
— LUST
— PRIVACY
— EROTICISM
— EXHIBITIONNISM
— POLITENESS
— DISCRETION
— GENITALS
— SEXUALITY
— GOOD MANNERS
— INTIMACY
— DESIRE
— FEAR
— EMBARRASSMENT
— RESERVE
— NUDITY
— SECRET
— SHAME
— PRUDISHNESS
— MORALITY
— RELIGION

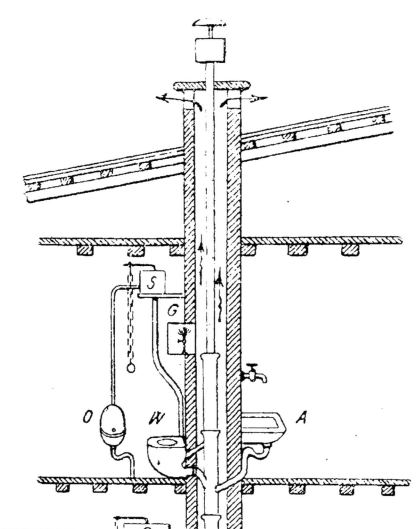

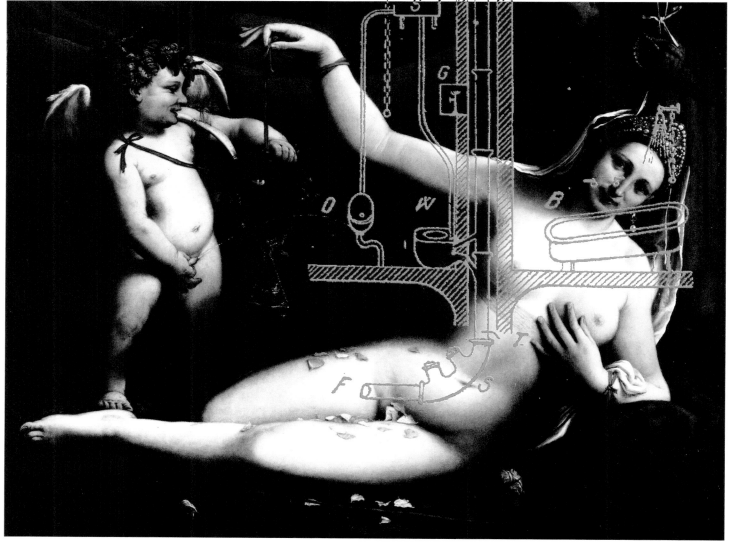

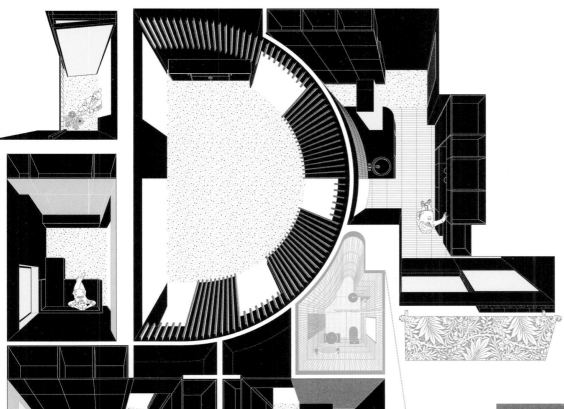

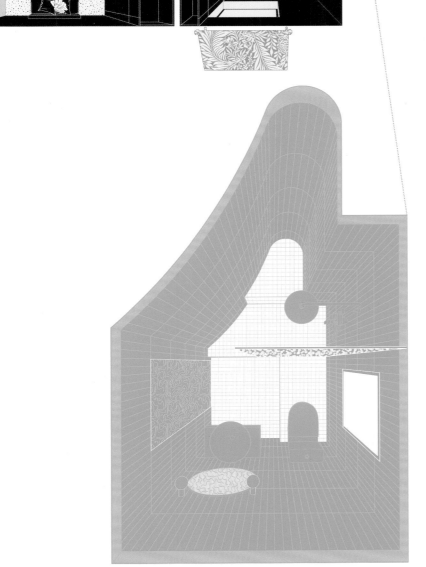

FORGOTTEN—LIKE THIS PARAPLUIE
AM I BY YOU FAITHLESS
BERNICE!

एक प्रेम कथा

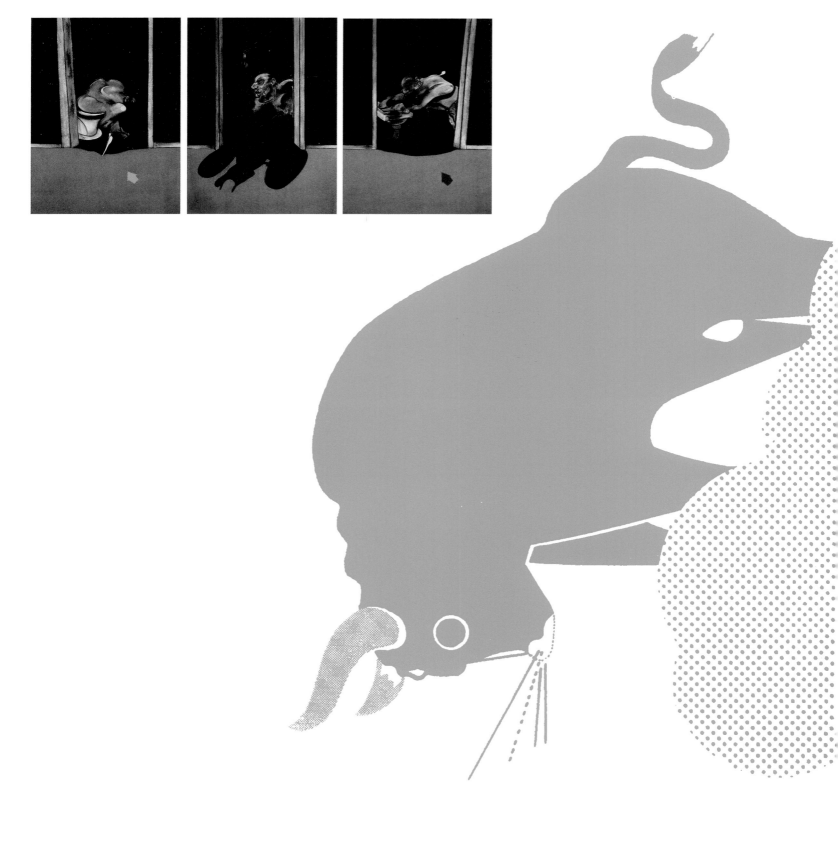

INSIDE
ROOMS
26 bathrooms
London & Oxfordshire
1985

Figure 4.6. Photograph of the Criterion Closet for Crane Co., c. 1936, designed by Henry Dreyfuss (American, 1904–1972). Henry Dreyfuss Collection, Cooper-Hewitt National Design Museum, Smithsonian Institution. Gift of Henry Dreyfuss, 1972.

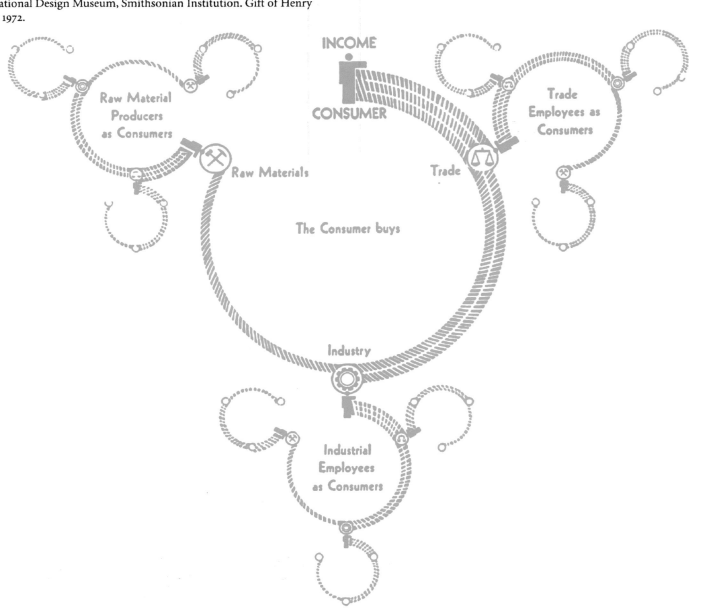

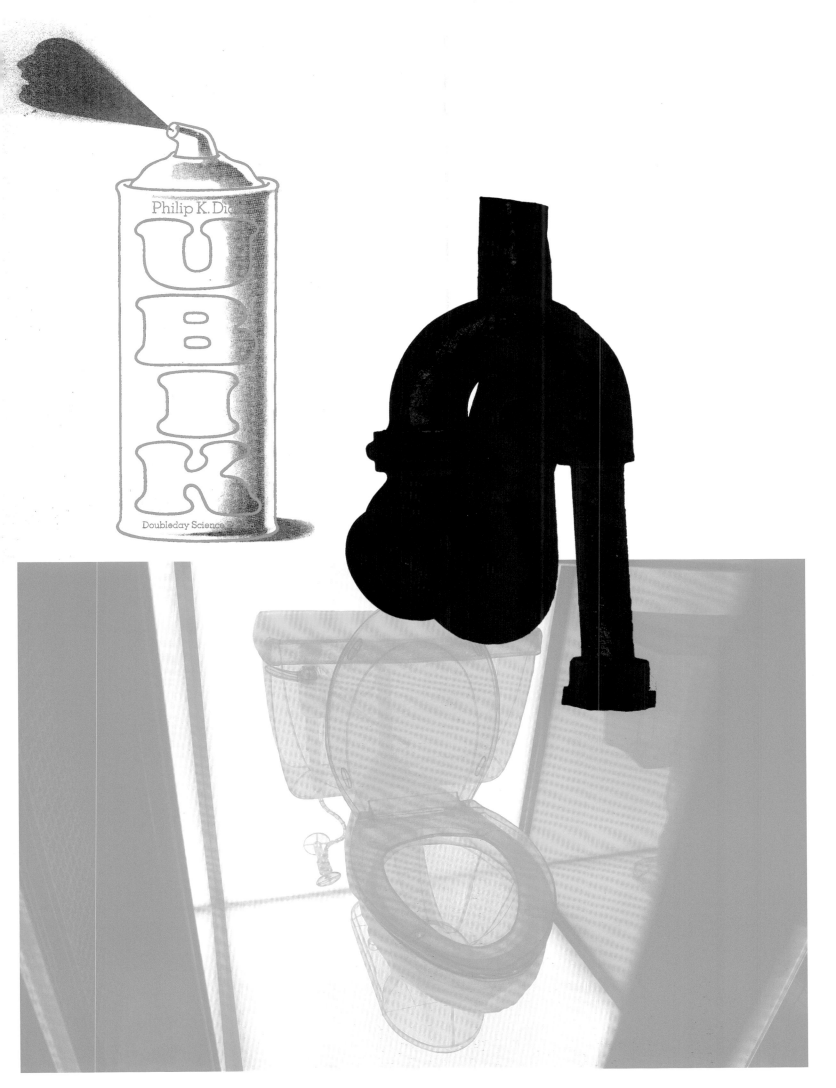

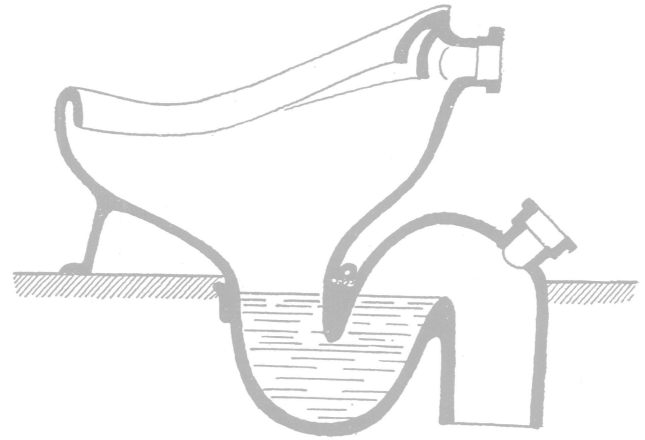

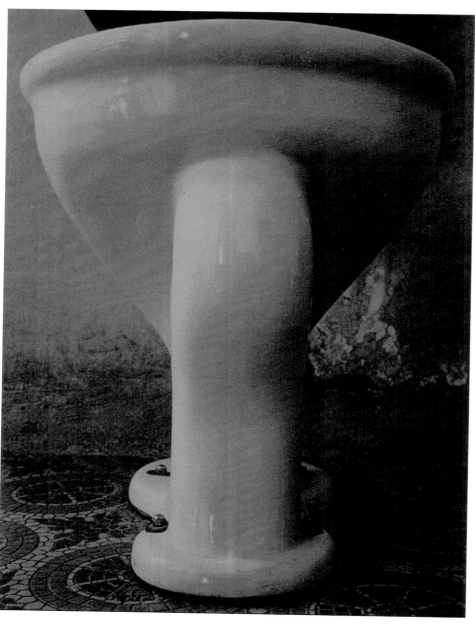

THE BLIND MAN

The Richard Mutt Case

They say any artist paying six dollars may exhibit.

Mr. Richard Mutt sent in a fountain. Without discussion this article disappeared and never was exhibited.

What were the grounds for refusing Mr. Mutt's fountain :—

1. Some contended it was immoral, vulgar.

2. Others, it was plagiarism, a plain piece of plumbing.

Now Mr. Mutt's fountain is not immoral, that is absurd, no more than a bath tub is immoral. It is a fixture that you see every day in plumbers' show windows.

Whether Mr. Mutt with his own hands made the fountain or not has no importance. He CHOSE it. He took an ordinary article of life, placed it so that its useful significance disappeared under the new title and point of view—created a new thought for that object.

As for plumbing, that is absurd. The only works of art America has given are her plumbing and her bridges.

"Buddha of the Bathroom"

.I suppose monkeys hated to lose their tail. Necessary, useful and an ornament, monkey imagination could not stretch to a tailless existence (and frankly, do you see the biological beauty of our loss of them?), .yet now that we are used to it, we get on pretty well without them. But evolution is not pleasing to the monkey race; "there is a death in every change" and we monkeys do not love death as we should. We are like those philosophers whom Dante placed in his Inferno with their heads set the wrong way on their shoulders. We walk forward looking backward, each with more of his predecessors' personality than his own. Our eyes are not ours.

The ideas that our ancestors have joined together let no man put asunder! In *La Dissociation des Idees*, Remy de Gourmont, quietly analytic, shows how sacred is the marriage of ideas. At least one charm-ing thing about our human institution is that although a man marry he can never be *only* a husband. Besides being a money-making device and the *one* man that *one* woman can sleep with in legal purity without sin he may even be as well some other woman's very personification of her abstract idea. Sin, while to his employees he is nothing but their "Boss," to his children only their "Father," and to himself certainly something more complex.

But with objects and ideas it is different. Recently we have had a chance to observe their meticulous monogomy.

When the jurors of *The Society of Independent Artists* fairly rushed to remove the bit of sculpture called the *Fountain* sent in by Richard Mutt, because the object was irrevocably associated in their atavistic minds with a certain natural function of a secretive sort. Yet to any "innocent" eye

Art in the Public Toilet

- public toilet not more in use
  - musealized
    - historical interiors adapted case by case to the art exhibition
    - it is itself a piece of art
  - abandoned
  - reconverted into art gallery
- public toilet in use
  - designed as a piece of art
  - adapted case by case to the art exhibition

Où sont les toilettes, s'il vous plaît ?

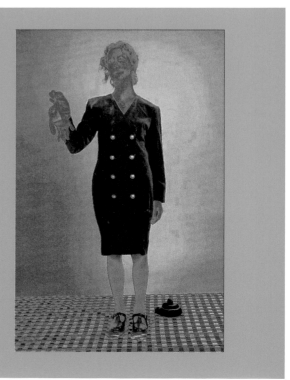

A Glimpse into Le Corbusier's Bathrooms
Andrés García Pruñonosa

In the context of an incipient realization by society that hygienic ideals were a necessity, the bathroom appeared as the most important contribution to the 20th century domestic program. (63) Oblivious to an ideal spatial configuration of the bathroom, architects and designers saw the bathroom as the prelude to the modernization of the home. They saw it as a testing ground, and it influenced their conception of the rest of the rooms in the house, allowing avant-garde architects to explore all the possibilities that would lead to the standardization of the bathroom. (64)

In many of Le Corbusier's works, the space for hygiene is a latent element in the operation of the home which, moreover, occupied a notable position inside the dwelling. The location of the sanitary core thus generated a link between the other domestic spaces of the house, in some cases encouraging ambiguity between their edges.

Le Corbusier's experimentation with bathroom design began with a modest example in *L'Esprit Nouveau*. This led him to investigate the room in his purist villas of the 1920s, where relaxation and hedonistic care of the body and life was shared happily by the family and their social environment, as it had been in ancient times.

From a transversal perspective of Le Corbusier's architectural work, we shall look at various bathrooms in 20th century houses in independent sections, focusing on their spatial impact on the overall distribution of the domestic program. In some cases, they are compared with contemporary work by other architects such as Eileen Gray,

63   María Carreiro and Cándido López, *La casa: piezas, ensambles y estrategias* (Málaga: Recolectores Urbanos, 2016), 141.   64   Ellen Lupton, Abbott Miller, *El cuarto de baño, la cocina y la estética de los desperdicios: Procesos de eliminación* (Madrid: Celeste, 1995), 25–38.

Pierre Charreau, and Auguste Perret, with whom Le Corbusier felt an degree of affinity or closeness. In this way, we shall see how the domestic machine, apparently relegated to the functional sphere, was in fact the precursor of the home layout.

The driving force behind this study, the involvement of the wet areas in the distribution of Le Corbusier's projects, is presented chronologically, with a more in-depth look at the repercussion of the bathrooms for the rest of the rooms in the house, the itineraries generated through them, and the ambiguity produced by their boundaries in the functions of the sanitary appliances.

L'Esprit Nouveau

At the International Exhibition of Modern Decorative and Industrial Arts in Paris (1925), Le Corbusier exhibited a full-scale prototype of a pavilion that he was promoting in the 1920s as a model of the modern home. No characteristic industrialized objects from an ordinary house were displayed in this pavilion, since Le Corbusier's intention was to avoid any reference to the personalized belongings of affluent houses. (65) Consequently, the sanitary appliances—mechanized by industry—"are exhibited as radiant works of art" (66) scattered through the bathroom.

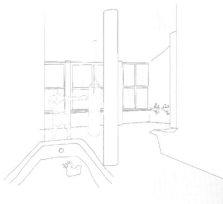

65   Willy Boesiger, Le Corbusier, Oscar Stonorov, *Le Corbusier et Pierre Jeanneret : œuvre complète,* vol. 1, 1910–1929 (Zurich: Les Éditions d'Architecture, 1937), 89.   66   "The Manual of the Dwelling", *Towards a New Architecture* (New York: Dover Publications, 1986), 122–123.

In this L'Immueble Villa prototype, the hygiene devices and the gymnastics room jointly governed the operation of the bathroom for the benefit of the bodily care of its users. The bathroom space thus seems bigger since these hygiene devices rush towards the boundaries of the room, permitting a greater spatial ambiguity in the rest of the room. This way of distributing the toilet towards the corners is reminiscent of a resource used by Adolf Loos in his house in Vienna (1903), which set a central space in the living room where all the room's belongings were attached, leaving a larger area in the center of the house to be perceived as a stage, freely available for interpretation. Similarly, the bathroom in the L'Esprit Nouveau pavilion was enriched by the large centralized space left by the sanitary appliances, permitting a multitude of activities related to physical training, personal hygiene, or even completely unrelated to body care, given that there would be no limits to the functional concept of this space.

In addition to all this, there was the lack of doors to enclose the contents of the bathroom, leaving the sanitary appliances in full view to the astonished gaze of the public, making them an essential part of the exhibition. To underscore this spatial continuity, Le Corbusier exhibited the bidet in a circulation zone, sheltered by the curved partition but without any door to hide its shape. It seemed to want to be part of the second floor distributor, acting as just another item in the space.

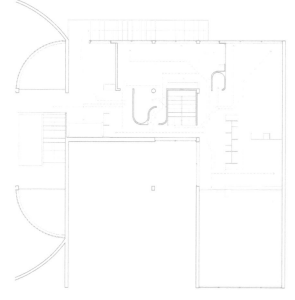

The L'Esprit Nouveau pavilion showed more clearly than ever before a bathroom fully incorporated into the private space of the master bedroom. Not only that, but it also allowed Le Corbusier to display his more personal nature and his more rational thinking about the construction of the house, exalting the ordinary objects of the everyday lives of the standard man, which sparked the interest of several entrepreneur clients.

Villa E-1027

The various phases that led designer Eileen Gray to build Villa E-1027 spanned the five years between 1924 and 1929. This home in Cap Martin, a village in the Maritime Alps of Nice, left Le Corbusier in awe, not only of the meticulous design of the interiors and exteriors as of the furnishings that she used.

Jean Badovici, Eileen Gray's partner at the time, encouraged the famous Parisian designer to dabble in the world of architecture by building this house. The French waterfront dwelling, like Le Corbusier's 1925 Decorative Arts pavilion, was an "intensely personal experiment in the progressive spirit of the Modern Movement." (67) Both were designed from the authors' deepest intimacy, revealing their personal character and manifesting their testaments as, "the legacy of their beliefs and convictions". (68) However, while Le Corbusier prioritized standardized objects

67   David Lluís López, "Eileen Gray: la emancipación femenina en la arquitectura moderna," *Dossiers Féministes*, no. 21 (Castelló: Universitat Jaume 1, 2016), 148.   68   Sung-Taeg Nam, "Los objetos sanitarios en Le Corbusier: La libertad dispositiva y la exposición radical en los años 20," *RA. Revista de Arquitectura*, no. 15 (Chile: Universidad de Chile, 2013), 93.

over personalized designs, Eileen Gray chose to design the furnishings for her home herself. Visually, the counterpoint to the furniture decoration was not only obvious on the "piano nobile", but also in the sanitary fixtures in the bathrooms. In the *L'Esprit Nouveau* pavilion, Le Corbusier resorted to purely industrialized white objects, subordinating form to function. In contrast, Eileen Gray was more careful and concerned with the shape of her sanitary appliances. These "machines" were not strictly pure, with different shades of colors and tiles used on walls of the room, which gave it more spatial warmth.

Indeed, Eileen Gray seems to have been a pioneer in the field of bathroom decoration. She employed ceramic tiles in different colors, and even invented an orange toilet seat for a context where white was still considered necessary to maintain an image of hygienic cleanliness. (69) This discrete gesture in her bathrooms exploded in the 1950s and 60s, raising the decoration of those rooms to the highest level. During those years, "the bathroom stopped being regarded as a machine room, and became another room in the house, where the sanitary ware became another piece of furniture in a totally different environment". (70)

69   Le Corbusier, "The Manual of the Dwelling," *Towards a New Architecture* (New York: Dover Publications, 1986), 122–123.   70   Justo García Navarro, Eduardo de la Peña Pareja, Fundación Cultural COAM, *El cuarto de baño en la vivienda urbana* (Madrid: Fundación Cultural COAM, 1998), 148.

Villa Le Lac

With a previously defined project under his arm, Le Corbusier found a plot of land on the edge of Lake Leman which seemed to be just waiting for the arrival of his parents' house. (71) In this project (late 1924), the bathroom is relegated to the end of the house, seen from the dining room as a background perspective. The washbasin became the protagonist of the scene, showing Le Corbusier's clear intention to clearly focus on "secondary" objects. (72) Alongside these sanitary fixtures, Le Corbusier added a dressing room at the end of the floor and two doors that connected the laundry room to the hygienic space of the house through a closet. This simple gesture permitted a ring-like circulation through all the rooms. As Josep Quetglas Riusech explains in "Cómo se construye una casita," "The ring is continuous: hall, living room, bedroom, toilet, closet, laundry room, kitchen, hall [...] There is a correlation between all the rooms, which follow each other hand-in-hand, like Matisse's circles of dancers". (73)

In the light of this connection, we can sense that there is a pre-established rhythm in the project design, influenced by the way the house was inhabited: the mother wakes up in her bedroom, does her personal hygiene and continues her route to the wardrobe, where she gets dressed. She then continues her journey to the laundry area to

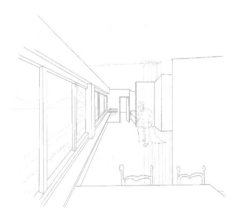

71   Le Corbusier, *Une Petite Maison 1923* (Buenos Aires: Infinito, 2005), 11.   72   Álvaro Antón Torres and Luis Martínez Santa-María, *WC. Algunos casos de estudio*, (Madrid: Escuela Técnica Superior de Arquitectura de Madrid, 2018), 39.   73   Josep Quetglas Riusech, "Cómo se construye una casita", *Le Corbusier, mise au point* (Valencia: General de Ediciones de la Arquitectura, 2012), 203.

leave her clothes. She turns right and enters the kitchen. There, like every morning, she makes breakfast, which she would then eat in the dining room.

It therefore seems reasonable to claim that the concatenation of small pieces with different roles, linked by a spatial continuity, permits a more versatile operation of the home. (74) Precisely in these rooms of the house, there is no intentional unity of different activities at the same time and the same place, but rather a breakdown of the functions into small precincts, interlinked for better fluidity. In addition, the spatial relationship created between the living room and the bathroom is enriched by the visual continuity through the window and the window sill, which integrate toilet, sink, and bathtub into the space as just additional objects in the room.

Finally, the ceramic tiling for the servants' areas in this house also stands out. It seems that Le Corbusier preferred not to draw it, and therefore not to build it in the realm of the bathroom, where the floor from the rest of the rooms enters following the longitudinal direction of the window sill. The sanitary devices are thus more tightly integrated with the shared rooms of the house, so it makes sense to think that the barriers between the served and the server spaces are increasingly blurred in order to improve the practicality of the house. (75)

74   Pere Fuertes and Xavier Monteys, *Casa collage: Un ensayo sobre la arquitectura de la casa* (Barcelona: G. Gili, 2007), 52.   75   Ignacio Paricio Ansuategui and Xavier Sust, *La vivienda contemporánea: programa y tecnología* (Barcelona: ITEC, 1998).

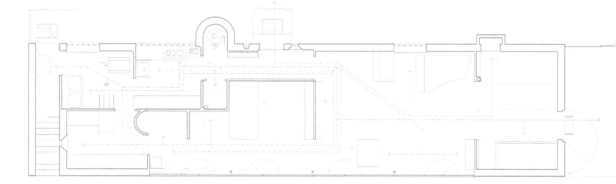

Villa Meyer

According to Tim Benton, one of the first draft designs for Villa Meyer explores the interior layout with the same degree of freedom and complexity as the free plan. It is drawn with the fine definition that could be expected of a definitive project. Le Corbusier submitted this version, dated April 21, 1926, to a much more organic spatial sub-division, independent of any compositional modulation that might regenerate the connection between the different uses. On the second floor of this version, the Meyer bathroom is aligned along the front wall next to the nanny's small washroom and the son's bathroom. Over two-thirds of the house frontage is thus dominated explicitly by the sanitary devices, in in a continuous, uniform interpretation of the "main" rooms of the house. A long window spans both the "noble" and the service rooms of the house, without any kind of distinction. (76)

The shape of the Meyer bathroom, connected to the master bedroom, is dilated by extending the sanitary fixtures beyond their profile. The bathtub (77) is pushed diagonally towards the enveloping wall, reshaping the boundaries of the bathroom and therefore of Mme Meyer's bedroom as well. The pivoting shape of this partition, described by Le Corbusier as a "grand piano", produces a continuous flow from the entrance to the apartment that guides and accompanies visitors as they walk in. Although this wall is depicted as a solid element in the floor plan of the April

76 Raúl Castellanos Gómez, *Plan Poché* (Barcelona: Fundación Caja de Arquitectos, 2012), 250–251. 77 A bath which, when turned diagonally, generates a spatial revolution, not only of the sanitary room of the rest of the space as well. Sung-Taeg Nam, "Los objetos sanitarios en Le Corbusier: La libertad dispositiva y la exposición radical en los años 20," *RA. Revista de Arquitectura*, no. 15, 2013, 93. 78 María Candela Suárez, "Las villas Meyer y Hutheesing-Shodhan de Le Corbusier," (Barcelona: Universitat Politécnica de Catalunya, 2007), 68. 79 Fuertes and Monteys, *Casa collage*, 34–36.

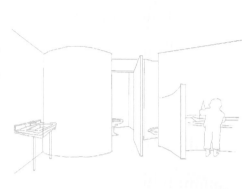

21 version, in the interior perspective of the bedroom we see that the wall does not touch the ceiling, with the two pieces merging spatially.

In contrast, the following version dated June 11, 1926 merges the rooms for the nanny and the baby into a single unit. (78) The bathroom acts as a link between the child's bedroom, the playroom, and the nanny's bedroom. They are positioned in the center of the apartment, permitting the spatial continuity of the three pieces that merge in the bathroom.

There are no limits to the use of these objects, since the concatenation of the playroom, the bathroom, and the child's bedroom gives rise to endless activities and fun games that sometimes only children are able to invent.

"Children are masters of the 'misuse' of the widest variety of things they can play with, and sometimes they naively bring out the "alter ego" of many objects and places in the house. Children teach us the ambiguity of many things by daring to use them in a different way [...] They barge into domestic architecture in a modern way and provide a different perspective on the house." (79)

The wild imagination of Meyer's son was thus able to evoke a fun game in the actual bathtub, sailing across the rough seas on a tiny boat.

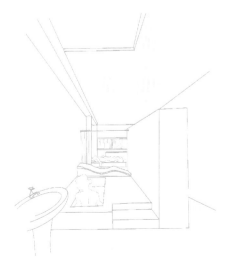

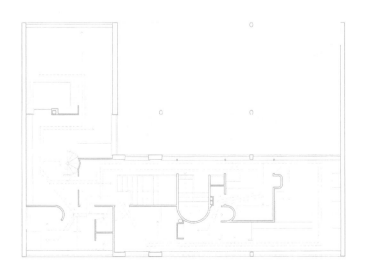

This room is a clear vindication of the bathroom as the nerve center of the house. It triggers a series of functional and spatial relationships through the house which provide versatility and ambiguity to even the most prosaic activity.

Villa Savoye

On April 12, 1929 Le Corbusier submitted his definitive proposal for Villa Savoye, to be built on Beauregard plateau in Poissy, following several designs that had been rejected by the clients. In this project, the bathroom is directly connected to the couple's bedroom, shown undisguised just a few centimeters away from the main room.

The figure of the washbasin and its stand, with a prominent presence seen from the entrance to the apartment, reappears without any misgiving, manifested all the more eloquently in the absence of enclosures that could hide its silhouette. In addition, a skylight above the washbasin exalts and magnifies its curved profile, a subtle action that manifests its position, as if it were a sacred relic beneath the great divine light.

Beside this object, there is a submersion bathtub that stands out from the rest of the sanitary ware. Turquoise blue glazed tiles cover the entire platform in which it is sunk, even perhaps substituting the sanitary ware since

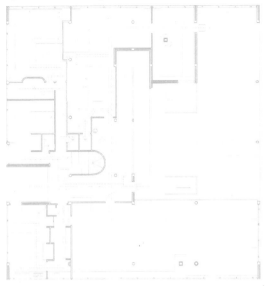

its continuity permits its use around the bathtub. (80) The link between the sanitary ware and the double bed is plausible thanks to the lack of partitions around these sanitary devices, the only element that might hide them if greater privacy was required being a two meter high white cloth curtain. (81)

A serpentine object that one might expect to find in a relaxation spa emerges perpendicular to the bathtub platform, organizing the two rooms. This is characteristic *chaise longue* silhouette used by Le Corbusier, Pierre Jeanneret, and Charlotte Perriand, (82) clad with black ivory tiles. Its shape and its position in the most intimate space of the house is an obvious vindication of the desire for well-being and personal relaxation through body care. (83) Its position between the bathroom and the bedroom inspires an unquestionable functional relationship, where Eugénie Savoye, after a relaxing bath, could lie on the *chaise longue* while chatting with her husband, who might be lying on the bed. This room is thus once again enriched by a versatility of functions that can be combined in their everyday use with the bedroom and the rest of the rooms in the apartment, illustrating the way the bathroom was no longer regarded as a uniform space with unvarying contents. (84) Le Corbusier showed that a plethora of disparate objects could burst in, inducing the functional plurality of body care.

The bathroom for the couple's son Roger, shared with the guest bedroom, is subject to a radial circulation structure that permits fluctuating passage through three adjoining doors. This presents an opportunity to take advantage

80   Anatxu Zabalbeascoa, "Baño," *Todo sobre la casa* (Barcelona: Gustavo Gili, 2011), 38.   81   Sung-Taeg Nam, *The Effect of Everyday Objects*, 96.   82   The evolution of the female bath in particular, as well as courtesy rules, allow new activities. Past bath spaces are old-fashioned; a new furniture's era starts. Boesiger, Le Corbusier and Stonorov, *Le Corbusier et Pierre Jeanneret*, 157.   83   Gonzalo Pardo Díaz, *Cuerpo y casa: hacia el espacio doméstico contemporáneo desde las transformaciones de la cocina y el cuarto de baño,* (Madrid: Universidad Politécnica de Madrid, 2016), 183–184   84   Sung-Taeg Nam, *The Effect of Everyday Objects*, 45.

of the position of these three elements to enhance the functional relationships of the rooms. (85) By the mid-20th century, this intention to unify served and servant spaces through interconnected doors had become a fairly common device for American architects. (86) However, in conjunction with the duality of the circulations, Le Corbusier was able to generate a completely different concept of flexibility from today's established concept. He employed the total permeability of the spaces, which in this case, facilitated more versatile routes and also an alternative use of the bathroom during the day, allowing different people to use the sanitary devices in different ways.

Maison de Verre

The novelty of the translucent glass used on the facade of this home was an innovation. The numerous mechanisms and gadgets, meticulously studied and detailed by avant-garde architect Pierre Chareau, aroused Le Corbusier's interest, who closely followed its construction near his studio. (87) These engineering systems made the Dalsace family's activity more relaxed, reflected in the many rooms devoted to personal hygiene. Each of these rooms is different from the others, since their character and their materiality respond to different intimate conditions, depending on the person who will enjoy the cleansing activity. (88)

85   Fuertes and Monteys, *Casa collage*, 78.   86   Randolph Williams Sexton, *American Appartment Houses of Today: Illustrating Plans, Details, Exteriors and Interiors of Modern City and Suburban Apartment Houses Throughout the United States* (New York: Architectural Book Publishing co., 1926).   87   The owner, Annie Dalsace, mentions her realisation that a small man stopped regularly in the hall to watch the construction and take notes. That man was none other than Le Corbusier. Jorge Torres Cueco, *Le Corbusier: Visiones de la técnica en cinco tiempos* (Barcelona: Fundación Caja de Arquitectos, 2004), 147. Original version: Marc Vellay, "Agli estremi del mattone Nevada," *Rassegna*, no. 24, December 1985, 16.   88   Hugo Losman, "On toilets and modernity—an interview with Mary Vaughan Johnson," *Paper (Platform for Architectural Projects, Essays & Research*, 2015).

Looking more closely, we can distinguish two different aspects of the Dalsace family's multipurpose bathroom. On the one hand, sheltered by an enigmatic system of metal cabins, Mr. Dalsace's sanitary equipment is hidden in a space with a more masculine character, where the most important feature is the shower function, a symbol of male sporting virility. On the other hand, Annie Dalsace's bathtub is separated from these sanitary appliances by folding shutters. In a similar context, each member of the couple could enjoy their body care in their own respective hygienic cabins. The adjacency of their sanitary facilities aided relaxed conversations, while the folding metal panels ensured privacy when required. (89) This aspect was also employed in the Savoye couple's rooms in the form of the tiled chaise longue and white curtain. However, while the Savoye apartment used a unique, uniform interpretation of the bedroom and the bathroom, in the Dalsace family's rooms, there was no such formal unit that could allow both rooms to be clustered in a single distributive piece. The purely functional nature of the bathroom is evidenced by the five entrance doors to this particular room, permitting versatile circulation in the midst of the wet area core. In spite of these obvious similarities, the spatial relationships that are defined are thus completely different in these two late-1920s homes, used by both architects as "laboratory space for experimentation". (90)

The couple's apartment is connected to the bedrooms, which have a private toilet, a washbasin, and a bidet. Inserted on one side of the room on a rectangular platform, these sanitary facilities are hidden behind fretted metal

89   Esther Da Costa Meyer et al., *Pierre Chareau: Modern Architecture and Design* (New York: The Jewish Museum; New Haven: Yale University Press, 2016), 180.   90   Hugo Losman, "On toilets and modernity."

panels whose transparencies leave little to one's imagination. These mobile concealment devices turn the bedrooms into a dramatic scene of theatrical performance. They can be compared to the *paravents* that muffled the actors' costume changes in theater dressing rooms, likewise sanitary appliances placed on the stage as the protagonists wait for the start of the performance.

These devices for bodily hygiene do not appear only in the bedrooms. In their daughter's bedroom, camouflaged by a folding wardrobe, a bathtub appears amidst her bookshelves. A bathtub thus resumes the leading role when the metal curtain is raised, its shape welcoming her figure for the duration of the act. These concealing devices play a new role here as a perfect hideout during the game.

In this paradigm of *spatial fluidity* (91) which enshrines the sanitary devices, Chareau's undeniable concern for the daily habits of the bourgeoisie was thus undeniably translated into a modernized vision of sanitary materiality and technique. Their shape projects a foretaste of the most avant-garde models of bathrooms blended with private rooms. (92)

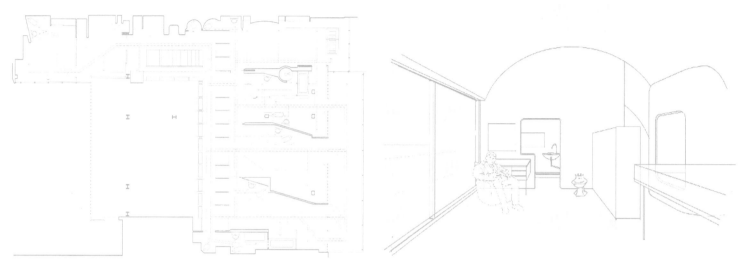

INTIMACY EXPOSED   Down the Hall to the Right? A Glimpse into Le Corbusier's Bathrooms   Andrés García Pruñonosa

Immeuble Porte Molitor

On June 28, 1931 a Parc des Princes real estate company contacted Le Corbusier to commission an apartment block on in Rue Nungesser-et-Coli, including the top part of the building for an apartment of his own. This project could be compared to the purist villas with gardens that he designed in the 1920s.

In the final version built in 1934, Le Corbusier detached the bidet from the closet where the other sanitary appliances were clustered, and placed it in the foreground of the room. This position was by no means arbitrary. Flora Samuel explains in her book *Le Corbusier in Detail* that the bidet's exhibition here is an expression of architect's antagonism to the Christian faith for its repression of the vanity of sex. (93) A guest seated at the dining table could thus admire Le Corbusier's bold decision to highlight an object of bodily purification with the backdrop of the bedroom in perspective. It was showing the guests its role in the body cult ceremony. (94)

The washbasin, which gravitates before the patented Nevada cobblestone wall, is another crucial item in this apartment. Full of pipes, ducts, and downspouts, its shape is interpreted as a metaphor for the organism that breathes life into the workings of the house. (95) This beating, throbbing organ supplies the indispensable elements to this inhabitable machine.

91   Raúl Castellanos Gómez, *Casa por casa: reflexiones sobre el habitar* (Valencia: General de Ediciones de Arquitectura, 2009), 76.   92   Carreiro, *La casa*, 153.   93   Flora Samuel, *Le Corbusier in Detail* (Amsterdam: Elsevier, 2007), 189.   94   His wife, Yvonne, was not exactly pleased about this decision. However, she put up with it. Charles Jencks, *Le Corbusier and the Continual Revolution in Architecture* (New York: Monacelli Press, 2000), 191.   95   Arthur Rüegg, "Transforming the bathroom: Perriand and Le Corbusier, 1927–57," *Charlotte Perriand: An Art of Living* (New York: Harry N. Abrams, 2003), 116.

Viewed as a whole, one of the most striking aspects of this version are textured lines on all the floors. This apparent massiveness invades the house from the equipment rooms. Each tiny part of the rooms in the house thus helps to create a single interpretation of the whole space. This could be regarded as the architect's iron determination to emphasize the dominance of the sanitary devices, which rush towards the rest of the rooms, imposing themselves as the precursors of spatial fluidity.

Immeuble d'Habitation Rue Raynouard

In 1928, Perret exhibited his skillful research concretely with the construction of a building on Rue Raynouard in the western part of Paris. He built his own private apartment on the seventh floor.

Auguste Perret placed his sumptuous bathroom in the south-eastern part of the apartment, along with the bedrooms and the living room. This position was relevant with respect to the rest of the servant spaces, since it was beside the most noble rooms in the house, and its orthogonal shape gave it the best views, directing the viewer's gaze across the privileged scenery of the Champ de Mars park. (96)

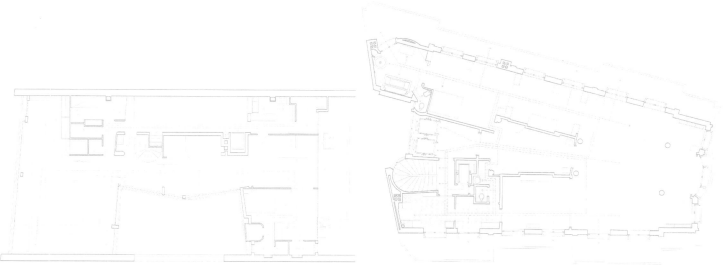

In contrast, the bathroom in the Molitor apartment was the result of the industrialized production of standard sanitary appliances, a powerful example of the artistic potential of these free organisms which spilled across the bedroom boundary, demonstrating their autonomy in the space. (97) Quite the opposite of Perret's building skills, here the result is a balanced bathroom, where he was even able to add a touch of color and materiality to each element.

But not everything is contrasted in these two apartments. Both show an obvious analogy with the bedroom as a nexus between the bathroom and the "living" rooms of the house. The spatial fluidity of both dwellings is tangible in the rooms stitched by the concatenated connecting doors, which blur the boundaries between the served and servant rooms. (98) However, although the relationship in Rue Raynouard between the three rooms is much clearer and direct due to the strong axial line of the plan, in the Molitor apartment, there is more equality between the bathroom and the noble rooms of the house thanks to the ceramic tiles, which provide a homogeneous reading to the house as a whole, whereas Perret's design is attenuated by the different types of paving.

Another highlight in the comparison between these two bathrooms is the similar attitude of both architects to the sanitary appliances. While Perret chose to feature the concrete washbasin as a perspective background for the dining room, Le Corbusier opted to exhibit the figure of the bidet, perhaps because of its more provocative intimate

96   Karla Britton, *Auguste Perret* (London: Phaidon, 2001), 146.
97   Sung-Taeg Nam, *The Effect of Everyday Objects*, 95.   98   José Ramón Alonso Pereira, "Perret & Piacentini. Análisis comparativo de dos arquitecturas paralelas," *VLC arquitectura*, vol. 4, no. 1, 14.

connotations. Although the anatomy of the washbasin is much more exposed than the bidet due to its central position on the axis of the house, Perret's basin is more restrained since it is not independent of the bathroom in the manner of Le Corbusier's bidet.

Whatever the case, despite the material disparity of the sanitary appliances and the discrepancies between the two bathrooms, both master and disciple obviously wanted to exalt the curved figures of these sanitary machines and exhibit them unashamedly to views through the doors of the rooms.

Conclusion

After the end of the 1920s, the bathroom became just as normal in home design as the bedroom. In this context, their impact was moderated and they began a constantly evolving transformation towards the embellishment of their spaces. (99)

Once the bathroom had become domesticated, the time had come for it to be regarded more in terms of design and personalization to the client's tastes, evolving towards the scenario of bodily comfort and greater flexibility. (100)

Although the characteristic machine-like aesthetics of the bathrooms in Le Corbuiser's purist villas were left behind,

99   Carreiro, *La casa*, 145.   100   Carreiro, *La casa,* 145.

it became clear that the Franco-Swiss architect's ideals about well-being and the functional bathroom had anticipated the designs that began to emerge in the second half of the 20th century, in which one could also sense an ineluctable concern for the satisfaction of the physical and bodily needs of the modern man.

It is true that there was no serious concern for bathroom aesthetics. Le Corbusier preferred industrialized shapes and the apparent coldness of his sanitary appliances over the warmth of the more refined designs proposed by Elieen Gray and Auguste Perret. Nevertheless, the very sobriety of these bathrooms exalted their comfort and relaxation-related aspects, like the bathrooms in houses designed later on in the 1950s and 60s with their large gym zones, spa-related objects and living rooms anticipated in designs like Villa Savoye and the Pavillon de L'Esprit Nouveau. Nor were these bathrooms to remain bound to the purely utilitarian nature of their core purpose. They seemed to project an image of continuous functional "flexibility," despite the fact that their distributive response was not marked by adaptable elements that could fold or slide out of the way. Nevertheless, their organizational principles gave rise to versatile uses and a multiplicity of circulation routes that were equally or even more consistent with the apparent flexibility generally found in these mobile elements.

Their approaches were obviously a different way for these architects to express flexibility, since they considered these rooms more in terms of their potential as a paradigm of fluidity and spatial dynamism produced through their correlation with the adjacent rooms. This relationship often gives rise to a spatial continuity that contributes to a valuable ambiguity in the boundaries of the bathrooms, where this functional variability is accepted in the daily life of the individuals and their versatile use of the house.

All this was feasible thanks to the combined and concatenated layout of the bathroom with the "living" rooms of the house. The itineraries that emerged in the middle of these rooms had some sort of an impact on the operation of the domestic program, offering a duality of circulations through the bathrooms that encouraged a sense of circulatory freedom and, in turn, consolidated a useful ambiguity through the interconnected rooms.

Ultimately, Le Corbusier, Eileen Gray, Pierre Charreau, and Auguste Perret opted for a design process in which the bathroom became a latent element in the domestic program of the house due to its involvement in the operation of the home, which essentially promoted the improved performance of the machine for living in the service of its users.

SPOT ON

Josiane Imhasly

The Alte Fabrik in the Swiss town of Rapperswil was virtually predestined for an exhibition on the subject of toilets. This building, now a cultural center, housed Geberit AG's first major production facility. The company is known not only in Switzerland but throughout Europe and beyond as a sanitary technology group that is now active worldwide. It can be traced back to the Gebert family from Rapperswil and Albert Gebert, who commissioned this old factory, the "Alte Fabrik".

Back in 1905, the Geberts succeeded in manufacturing the first lead-lined wooden cisterns. The *à Phönix*, which was protected by the Imperial Patent Office in 1912, was produced for several decades, with subsequent innovations that significantly improved toilet flushing. The importance of reliable toilet flushing can hardly be overestimated to this day. Few people have never found themselves in the unpleasant situation of being confronted with someone else's "business" in a toilet (à Florian Bühler, Abort, 2019). This is precisely where fear of the other emerges, as Ruth Barcan notes: "When I hear of people afraid to touch a tap, I think less of real germs than of the fear of the other" (101). This physical contact is just one of the many complexes and sensitive relationships with and in this place. The toilet is a multi-layered cultural form in which psychology, medicine, sociology, architecture, design, and technology are intertwined. In the *Spot on* exhibition, the toilet stands out as a metaphor and interface for the inside and the outside, the visible and the invisible. What was just an invisible part of

101   Molotch, Harvey, Laura Noren, eds. *To Toilet: Public Restrooms and the Politics of Sharing*. (New York: NYU Press, 2010).

the human being turns into something disgusting: a visible excretion in the toilet bowl, to be immediately ejected and disappear into the sewer pipe and the sewage system. The toilet brings the inside of a person—her or his biology and psyche—into contact with the outside, their environment, the architecture. Moreover, it is connected to the underground via the invisible sewage system.

The use of a toilet can thus also be understood as a moment of transfer: on the one hand as an interface between the visible and the invisible in our society, and on the other hand, as a precarious psychological moment.

More than 50 years ago, Alexander Kira's study *The Bathroom* (102) showed that the normal posture used in the West for defecation is harmful to our health. Yet the design of the toilet and the associated posture has hardly changed since then. "Toilets resist change," notes Harvey Molotch in the Introduction to *Toilet: Public Restrooms and the Politics of Sharing* (103), because the designers of toilets plan for them to be hidden: the toilet is also a taboo for architects. This tabooing of human excretion, a relatively recent phenomenon, has advanced hand in hand with modernization. Using the toilet, theories of modernization can be questioned as theories of progress. Toilets with flushing water existed as early as 3000 BC, and in the Roman Empire, there were even latrines with underfloor heating and marble seats. In the Middle Ages, however, they were dispensed with and the urge for relief shifted to the street. According to Norbert Elias (104), the tabooing of the excretory functions has had something to do with the process of civilization since the 18th century, i.e., in step with changes in

social structures. In Purity and Danger (105), Mary Douglas argues that dirt is what society defines as such in order to maintain order.

At the level of the individual as well, the toilet represents a psychologically critical moment. One has to deal with one's own body and its uncontrollable expressions, as well as those of other people. As soon as the excretion is ejected, it is no longer considered to belong to the body. It stands for an encounter with the repressed and the threat of non-influenceable transformation.

A key work of the exhibition is Sarah Lucas' sculpture *The Old In Out* (1998). In this work, the toilet, a potentially disgusting object, becomes an extremely attractive sculpture cast from polyurethane. This was originally part of an installation consisting of nine toilets. The ordinary becomes elegant here, as is so often the case in Lucas' work. The English expression "the old in-out" has both sexual and—in this case—scatological connotations. It reminds one of foods and liquids that enter the body and are expelled as excretion. The transparency of the sculpture also points to what flows through the body. The toilet motif is repeated in the work of Lucas, one of the major representatives of Abject Art. This feminist art movement deals with abjection, things that trigger disgust or phobias. With Lucas, toilets stand for mortality, self-destructive instincts, and abusive attitudes towards the female body.

102 Alexander Kia, *The Bathroom* (Ithaca: Cornell University, 1966). 103 Molotch, Harvey, Laura Noren, eds, *Toilet: Public Restrooms and the Politics of Sharing* (New York: NYU Press, 2010). 104 Elias, Norbert, *The Civilizing Process, Vol.I. The History of Manners* (Oxford: Blackwell, 1969), 224–236. 105 Mary Douglas, *Purity and Danger* (New York: Praeger, 1966).

The Old In-Out is also reminiscent of the most famous toilet in art history, Duchamp's 1917 *Readymade Fountain*. On the one hand, the aesthetic exaggeration of the object, the toilet bowl or urinal, is achieved by *Fountain*, through the title and in *The Old In-Out*, the material and the design. On the other hand, the toilet is visible in both works as a gender-specific object. The urinal was ultimately not approved for exhibition by the Society of Independent Artists in New York in 1917 because above all, it was deemed not suitable to be presented to the female exhibition visitors. This gendered connotation is particularly interesting against the background of *Fountain* for Marcel Duchamp and also for a woman, Dada artist Elsa von Freytag-Loringhoven. Several art historians have provided credible evidence for this thesis in recent years. Glyn Thompson, for example, showed that the urinal was not in fact made by J.L. Mott Iron Works, as Duchamp claimed in the 1960s (in an interview with Otto Hahn: "Mutt came from Mott's"), (106) but by Trenton Potteries Co. Given that *Fountain* was sent to the Society from Philadelphia, and Baroness Elsa von Freytag-Loringhoven was living there at the time, her authorship seems be entirely plausible. Somewhat more daring is the interpretation of R. Mutt's signature as a reference to "mother"—the baroness came from Germany—or the statement that when turned 180 degrees, the urinal reminds one of a uterus. In response to these research results, ten artists—Anna Artaker, Julia Bodamer, Lily Cursed, Lotte Meret Effinger, Julia Kälin, Quintessa Matranga, Victorine Müller, Sereina Steinemann, Vanessa Thill and Addie Wagenknecht—were invited to pay homage to Elsa von Freytag-Loringhoven's *Fountain* to complement the umpteen homages to Marcel Duchamp's

Fountain and playfully capture the possibility of female authorship for this famous artwork. Posing the question, *Où sont les toilettes s'il vous plaît?* (2018), Bethan Huws pays an important tribute to Duchamp as well. Huws has been reflecting on Duchamp's work since 1999 and enriches the research about him with her own interpretation. In particular, at the linguistic level, titles, puns, ideograms and symbols have attracted her attention, along with Duchamp himself. The social environment in Duchamp's time was shaped by World War I (to which the Dada movement reacted): upheavals and revolutions, modernizations and industrialized production. This shows in a work like *Fountain*, as well as in the question of the relationship between art and industrial production that generally arises (107). The avant-garde of modernism was interested in technological modernization at the beginning of the 20th century, not as the standard bearer of this modernity but as its critic. It aestheticized modernity and showed that the ideology of progress was absurd and deceptive. Sewage systems and bathrooms have been shaped by this ideology of modernity and progress, like other areas of architecture. This aspect has been visiblized in the series *Ideal Standard* (2015) by Noha Mokhtar & Gregor Huber. Their photographic investigation of facades in the broader sense tracks down political ideologies and shows how they are manifested in architectural and domestic objects like the stacked toilets photographed by Mokhtar in Egypt in 2015. But wouldn't it be equally plausible if these toilets had been photographed in the USA in the 1960s? The words of Molotch come to mind: "Toilets resist change". (108) In 1966, Alexander Kira published *The Bathroom*. (109) This study was to the bathroom what

106   Hahn, Otto, "Passport No. G255300 [Interview with Marcel Duchamp]." *Art and Artists*, vol. 1, no. 4, July 1966, 7–11.   107   Boris Groys, "On Art Activism," *e-flux journal*, https://www.e-flux.com/journal/56/60343/on-art-activism/, last accessed September 5th, 2022.

the Kinsey Reports of 1953 were to the realm of sexuality: the first comprehensive scientific investigation of a social taboo. In view of the social upheavals at the end of the 1960s, it is not surprising that the first edition in 1966 contains schematic drawings and images of clothed bodies instead of photographs of naked people, which changed for the second edition, published in 1976. Perhaps the interdisciplinary Fluxus group of artists, built around George Maciunas on the issue of architecture and design issues, was inspired by Kira's study to formulate suggestions for alternative toilet designs that were not meant to be very serious (110). The Fluxus ideas in the 1970s, like at the design competition for the toilet of the future launched by Geberit AG in 1989, show that it is not that easy to design a "better" toilet. How design and technical solutions have changed over the last hundred years and the arguments used to sell the products sold to men (and less often to women) is illustrated by the wallpaper featuring Geberit advertisements and product information since the 1920s.

The design of sanitary appliances is in itself a challenge for private spaces. The task becomes even more complex when it comes to public toilet facilities. Only here are the taboos associated with the toilet completely broken down. Here, the boundaries between public and private become blurred, and psychological and social mechanisms of oppression become visible. Several works in the exhibition address the toilet as a social space with certain rules of behavior and a strict communication system. Public toilets are a particularly sensitive issue, as shown by the absurd discussions fueled by Donald Trump about transgender and gender-neutral toilets in recent years, because

they are gendered places. Jaanus Samma has been examining public men's toilets for several years. *The Readymade Divider* (2017) takes a central position in this area of his work. The three partition walls create—in the exhibition space as well—a stage on which a social theater takes place. They focus on contacts in the sphere of the urinal and the associated uncertainties. Samma's collages entitled *Study of a Toilet* (2016–2018) focus on overlooked objects with an unusual combination of historical ornaments and motifs, as well as everyday objects from toilets. The collages elevate these objects and expose their misguided tabooing.

Julie Verhoeven is a master at addressing taboo subjects with ease and humor in her art. In 2016, she transformed a public toilet facility as part of Frieze Projects at the London Fair into an immersive work of art called *The Toilet Attendance… Now Wash Your Hands*. She decorated the room, developed an ambient fragrance and played music mixed with digestive noises.

As a toilet attendant, Verhoeven sold toilet props such as pile of shit emojis made from velvet (customers were allowed to pay as much as they wanted), and engaged her toilet users in conversation. With her performances she drew attention to the precarious working conditions of the mostly female toilet attendants. As seen in the video *Now Wash Your Hands* (2016), she encountered various toilet taboos without fear of contact: menstruation, sex, excretions, drugs, and smells. In the video, the toilet attendants almost become psychologists who strike up conversations amongst themselves and with others on issues such as gender, disgust and hygiene.

108   Molotch, Harvey, Laura Noren, eds, *Toilet: Public Restrooms and the Politics of Sharing* (New York: NYU Press, 2010), 4.   109   Alexander Kia, *The Bathroom* (Ithaca: Cornell University, 1966)   110   Maciunas, *Flux Toilets* (New York City: Fluxus Newsletter, 1972).

The message, "Now wash your hands" is followed by *Vos mains ne présentent maintenantplus de risque* (2019) by Johana Blanc. Various subtly pronounced instructions for action on the toilet such as the request to wash one's hands or automatic flushing are intended to ensure that the toilet remains a bacteria-free precinct. Johana Blanc pursues such instructions on a verbal level. She condenses found requests to wash hands into poetic texts, which she applies manually by hand in lettering. This "contaminated" script implicitly refers to the contamination that one wishes to counter with hand washing. The soaps by Isabelle Krieg, Sonja Duò-Meyer, Mickry 3, Marlies Pekarek and TOILETPAPER are also linked to this topic and expand it in various directions. Soaps are multi-layered through their material. They have a special aesthetics and feel (one is inevitably reminded of Lucas' *The Old In-Out*) and, last but not least, they also refer to cleansing with soap as a global cultural technique. As objects midway between art and design, they enjoy great popularity.

Toilets are not only connected or related to bacteria. Standardized behavior is also expected here. Quantitatively-dosed soap dispensers, self-closing taps and timed hand dryers are the most harmless signs of this expectation. Steven Pippin defied this in his work, *The Continued Saga of an Amateur Photographer, dripping with English humor* (1993). He turned a train toilet into a camera obscura on a trip from London to Brighton. A video documents his actions, his performance, the way he exposes, develops, and fixes the photographic paper. Is the toilet becoming a viewing machine or is Pippin's work more a self-portrait? This reversal of perspectives is manifested

as one of the leitmotifs of the exhibition in two other works, Daniel Eatock's *Toilet Paper* (2019) and Andreas Slominski's *Cap* (2016). Both play with the bourgeois habit of hiding toilet paper in a witty way. But what is actually said about us in the fact that we equip toilet paper roll holders with mirrors so that we can see ourselves while we are sitting on the toilet (Florian Bühler, *Wandstück I*, 2017)?

The *Stoned in the Bathroom* installation by Jérôme Nager and Timéa Schmidt, from the Interior Architecture Department at HEAD – Genève, returns to the fact that deviant behavior in public toilets is not tolerated. Fluorescent lighting indicates a form of social and political oppression of marginalized groups in this place. These lights were installed in Swiss toilets at the beginning of the 1990s to make it impossible for drug addicts to see their veins and to ban them from these places. An essay by Nager follows the history of this lighting, and a sound track complements the installation with noises from the interior of the toilet technology. A transportation box indicates that the installation could be set up elsewhere at any time.

To close the circle—we remember questions of technology, design, and architecture in the haze of the toilet—we dare to suggest an allegory between the inside of the body and the inside of architecture with two works. Firstly, Jan Sebesta's work *Slepenec* (2019), which invites one to carry one of the four yellow tube or worm-like parts on the body. One can and should reach into these objects to activate a loudspeaker that makes digestive noises. Here, the proximity of infrastructure and body is not only visible, but can also be experienced.

Finally, *Kanalvideo* by Fischli//Weiss (1992) takes us on a hypnotic journey through the "guts" of the city of Zurich. The tracking shot is a cinematographic readymade of the sewage system. The artists assembled film material created by the urban drainage department and processed it with colored grids. Fischli//Weiss' preference for the repressed, the mundane, and the seemingly banal shows itself literally on the surface and is transformed. *Kanalvideo* can also be read as an ironic commentary on Switzerland, which is known for its cleanliness.

STONED IN THE BATHROOM
An Attempt to Control the Blue
Jérôme Nager

The title of this chapter, a nod at an underrated song in the history of American rock, refers to what at first sight seems anecdotal, but in fact is a very real problem. It has to do with the notion of our perception of space and the influence that it has on our mood. In fact, if Chubby Checker is "sitting in the bathroom one Sunday afternoon" (111) and it is so important to share with his listeners for a whole song, it is because there is a close connection that links drugs to toilets. Needless to say, drugs and public baths go hand in hand. To prove it, one merely has to combine these two keywords in the search bar of the *Le Temps* newspaper archive (112) to get more than 5,000 results. (113) Is this a fact or an unconscious reminiscence of the media coverage for this highly successful topic since the late 1980s? Although this question is reasonable, it will certainly remain unanswered. Nevertheless, the fact is that for thirty years, this connection has been anchored in the collective unconscious, perhaps much more in Switzerland than elsewhere, and that it has never stopped feeding debate.

111   Chubby Checker, *Stoned in the Bathroom*, Chubby Checkered, "Stone in the Bathroom," *Chequered!* (London: London Records, 1971).   112   *Le Temps* Archives, https://www.letempsarchives.ch/recherche?q=toilettes+%2B+drogue+apres%3A1920+avant%3A2004#, accessed April 9, 2019.   113   The *Le Temps* archives contain only three newspapers, *La Gazette de Lausanne*, *Le Journal de Genève* and *Nouveau Quotidien*, all of which are French-speaking. This result allows us to comprehend the magnitude of the subject dealt by the media.

To understand the extent of the demand and its source, we must go back in history. At the dawn of the 1960s, Switzerland did not seem far from its stereotypical image. It was peaceful, clean, hard-working and unharmed by the scourge of drugs that was to plague it two decades later. The authorities, victims of the ostrich syndrome, turned its back completely on the growing drug phenomenon until it emerged out of the shadows. It was only in the 1970s that Switzerland confronted the drug issue for the first time in a relevant way, in an era when the social movements emerging from the May 68-inspired liberation from customs became fashionable. (114) At a time when drug trafficking, but not consumption, was punishable, the authorities reacted, revised the Federal Narcotics Act, and suppressed even the simplest use of drugs. (115) Convinced that this was the only way to return to peace, the authorities were surprised to find it ineffective, since the sharply growing number of users, especially of heroin, did not stop. (116) Between the end of the 1980s and the beginning of 1990s, the large cities of Switzerland were confronted with a growing presence of drug addicts who chose various public spaces as their home. Media coverage brought the problem out of the shadows and gradually made it visible, greatly disturbing the authorities and the general population. In Zurich, where the phenomenon struck the hardest, the drug users occupying the Platzspitz numbered several thousand. (117) The growing presence of this population, the consequential drawbacks and the pressure exerted by local shopkeepers and residents pushed the authorities to evacuate the places and finally close the park. Considering the

114   Kim Carrasco, *Gouvernance de la politique drogue dans les villes suisses* (Master's thesis of Advances Studies (MAS) in Public Administration (Laussane: UNIL, 2016), 3.   115   "La politique suisse en matière de drogues: un modèle pionnier," *Spectra*, last modified April 2017, http://www.spectra-online.ch/fr/spectra/themes/la-politique-suisse-en-matiere-de-drogue-un-modele-pionnier-589-10.html.   116   Up to 30,000 people, in a 1990's estimate. Kim Carrasco, *Gouvernance*, 3.   117   "Up to 3000 Swiss and foreign drug addicts came to stock up, mainly on heroin". "Zurich évacuait, il y a 25 ans, la scène ouverte de la drogue du Platzspitz", *RTS Info*, https://www.rts.ch/info/regions/autrescantons/8361972-zurich-evacuait-il-y-a-25-ans-la-scene-ouverte-de-la-drogue-du platzspitz.html., accessed April 10, 2019,

fact that this decision was not supported by any accompanying measures, the drug addicts, deprived of their favorite place, naturally moved a few hundred meters away to the abandoned Letten station. Observation of what happened afterwards was bitter. It took very little time for this new scene to become even larger than the previous one, and it became the meeting place for several thousand people until the situation became almost uncontrollable. (118) These real-life scenes, unprecedented in the recent history of Switzerland, gradually became inevitable, even outside our borders, to the point of being perceived as the archetype of a zone of non-legality (119) that marked a turning point in the awareness of the Swiss authorities. The echo abroad was so great that even the US-based CNN produced a report on the problem in the early 1990s. (120) It had to reach the point that the image of Switzerland was affected and the of the concerns of the population were crystallization before the government sought a viable solution to fix the problem. This is how this awareness has paved the way for a new drug policy at the canton and federal levels. (121) Indeed, in just a few years, Switzerland adopted a "four-pillar" policy, based on prevention, therapy, risk reduction, and repression. (122) This policy has proven to be effective, particularly in reducing the number of overdoses. It has and still inspires the anti-drug policies of several foreign countries. Following these basic measures, open-air squats gradually disappeared and gave way to injection rooms. <u>Although the drug problem is still fundamentally unresolved and will probably never be resolved, at least it has been contained.</u>

118   *RTS Info*, "Zurich évacuait."   119   Kim Carrasco, *Gouvernance*, 3.
120   Kim Carrasco, *Gouvernance*, 3.   121   RTS Info, "Zurich évacuait."   122   *RTS Info*, "Zurich évacuait."

After presenting the scenario for this dark age in Swiss history, without any pun intended, we can talk about the side effects that these events have had on public infrastructures. They range from simple objects such as syringe barrels placed in toilets to other more drastic measures. Devices have abounded not to help the fight against drugs, but rather against their users. One such device, which may initially seem anecdotal, has been the proliferation of blue lights in public spaces, especially in toilets. Many people still ignore their purpose, but Switzerland, we have all suffered from them on some occasion.

It is impossible to find a clear answer to the question of who was behind the installation of these lights in public spaces (city centers, railway stations, shopping centers, discos, etc.), but we know for certain that it was not an architect or a designer. Since the Swiss administrative system is split up between federal, cantonal and municipal jurisdiction, the search for this source is utopian, above all because it is not a measure with established jurisprudence. The identity of the individual who had the brilliant idea that changing the color of light bulbs would prevent drug addicts from injecting themselves therefore remains a mystery. Let us imagine for a moment, in the context of today's compulsive need to find a culprit for every circumstance, that this idea came from an elected official, a deputy, a zealous functionary, or even a lambda citizen spurred by an almost humanistic desire to fight unflinchingly against the drug problem. One can easily imagine the mental process that led him to present such a proposal.

His starting point was undoubtedly the fact that there are too many undesirable drug addicts in public bathrooms and that they use these places for the specific purpose of taking drugs, thus depriving the good citizen of a public service infrastructure. So, he must have wondered how to prevent these miserable people from entering these places in the first place and shift their dirty activity away from the innocent view of the lambda person. Finally, it was probably the thought that these ungrateful people inevitably need to see their veins to satisfy their needs that triggered the ingenious idea: a light close to the color of their veins should be installed to make injection difficult or impossible.

Whatever the case, the goal of the person or people who initiated this measure was unquestionably to prevent addicts from being able to inject themselves in public places by making it much more difficult. The fact is that a blue-colored light in an enclosed space does prevent one from detecting superficial veins. This was expected to result in this population moving elsewhere. At the same time, it would also have the effect of rediscovering the original use of these public places by the users for whom they were originally designed, whose safety and well-being was the authorities' main concern.

The irony of this fate is that anyone who has once found themselves beneath this lighting undoubtedly has a memory of mixed feelings of resentment and strangeness. Who has never experienced a frantic search for a public

toilet due to an urgent need? Once this refuge for a little privacy is found, the relief is often accompanied by the desolation of having to sit in a place drowned in a glaucous environment tinged with blue where previous users have not failed to leave a memento of their presence. Initially, the purpose of these lights was not to cause unease among ordinary users, but that has been precisely one of its effects due to the lack of comfort that it produces. The legitimate question that can be asked is therefore whether this discomfort is at least offset by a solution to the problem that the lights were initially intended to solve.

Against all expectations, it is now proven that these blue lights do not fulfill their expectations. Worse still, that they have had a negative impact, since they pose more risks not only to the drug-dependent population but also to non-users of drugs. In fact, one study using testimonies from drug users has seriously questioned the effectiveness of blue lights installed in public places. (123) This study traces the feelings of people whose presence is not desired in toilets equipped with these lights. In the first place, the researchers found that public toilet injections were only an emergency solution for participants, since they clearly preferred private locations. Indeed, public toilets only offer relative privacy and questionable hygiene. Despite this, and because the ultimate need for injection takes precedence over any other consideration, public toilets are the ideal rescue solution, whether or not they have blue lights. The majority of respondents knew the purpose of the blue lighting, namely that it was an attempt to

123   Alexis Crabtree et al., "A qualitative study of the perceived effects of blue lights in washrooms on people who use injection drugs," *Harm Reduction Journal*, vol.10, no. 22, 2013.

impede drug use. Some of them, however, stated that the lights did not discourage them from using drugs, and more than half of the respondents said that by forcing drug addicts like themselves to move to other places where their consumption would be more visible, they felt deeply stigmatized.

Another publication describes in more detail the health risks posed by the presence of blue neon lights, (124) which in fact encourage more dangerous injections. Blue lights interfere with the perception of superficial veins such as those in the forearm, forcing drug users to try to inject into deeper veins such as the femoral vein that does not need to be visible. The medical risks then become serious: infection, thrombosis, lesions to the artery or the femoral nerve. Another risk induced by this lighting is that of missing a vein, overdosing the injection or administering the product in the surrounding tissues, all three scenarios being potentially fatal. (125)

These observations are only concerned with perceived and proven drug addicts. As mentioned above, modified lighting also has a negative impact on the use that every ordinary person can make of these blue spaces.

A space remains abstract as long as light does not manage to draw its contours and define its shape. The dimensions of a space are formed through light. Its quantity and its contribution shape our feelings because our sensations are largely defined by vision. Light, both natural and artificial, undeniably influences the effects and qualities of a space which, depending on the latter, appears to us in totally different ways.

124   Kevin Flemen, "Blue Light Blues: The Use of Coloured Lights as a Deterrent to Injecting" (*Kfx*, 2003)   125   Kevin Flemen, "Blue Light Blues."

Imposing such a measure on ordinary citizens forces them to use a diminished space, in the sense that some of the functions of a bathroom are denied to them. Not without reason, artist Bruce Nauman has repeatedly used blue light in his installations, especially in *Natural Light, Blue Light Room*, in order to deliberately disorient the audience and cause a sense of discomfort in it. (126) In less artistic contexts, this light is also known for its uncomfortable properties, if only for hindering simple gestures.

The effect of blue lighting undeniably hinders the use of a mirror, as it alters the viewer's perception. For example, it makes it impossible to see make-up, comb one's hair or even perceive one's reflection correctly. This has also had a real impact on the feeling of the space, since the mere sight of a blue light can cause anxiety and discomfort, especially in a closed, restricted location. In effect, it announces a pre-existing problem of drug addiction and therefore insecurity. Although this may be erroneous, it is nevertheless the way that the user, confronted with such lighting, will perceive things.

Why then, one may ask, should blue neon lights be installed if their utility is not proven? Conversely, such facilities are non-existent in places that are not plagued by the presence of drug addicts and are considered safe. In addition to influencing the feelings of ordinary users, this diffuse lighting also has the disadvantage of making these particular spaces less safe, since reduced vision in them can cause falls or injuries due to impact on

126   Joseph Ketner II, *Elusive Signs: Bruce Nauman Works with Light*, (Cambridge, Mass.: The MIT Press, 2006), 45.

dangerous objects. (127) In short, the installation of blue neon lights is unsatisfactory for drug users and also for ordinary citizens in terms of the use that each of these populations can make of public toilets. Even admitting, for argument's sake, that this design had worked to prevent drug addicts from using public washrooms, would the result have truly been satisfying in terms of the public interest? The blue lights that deter some drug users from shooting up in public toilets have not stopped their drug use or reduced their injections. (128) At most, the result has been the shift of the problem to less monitored areas such as stairways, car parks, secondary roads, parks, abandoned lots, etc., with all the associated implications. In fact, drug addicts prevented from using public toilets were forced to take possession once again of public parks like Platzspitz or Letten, which the authorities had worked so hard to avoid.

Today, the blue light trick is disappearing in Switzerland. In fact, consultation with the urban planning services of three major cities in Switzerland confirmed our suspicion that these lights were too ineffective to justify their continued installation. Furthermore, drug addicts have found a solution to inject themselves in this light as well, using the torch on their mobile phones to counteract the effect of the blue light waves. It is therefore surprising to note that although their relative ineffectiveness has finally been noted in Switzerland, the installation of blue lights is on the increase in other countries, particularly France (129) and the United States. (130)

127 Kevin Flemen, "Blue Light Blues," 3.   128 Kevin Flemen, "Blue Light Blues," 4.

Although this review has shown that this type of device does not have the desired efficiency, the fact remains that it continues to be used, and is even increasing in some countries. Furthermore, blue lights are by no means the only example of dissuasive devices whose purpose is to induce or control certain behavior. These are also known as defensive or hostile architecture. (131) This is "the art of designing buildings, public spaces or equipment to exclude unwanted use," (132) a term that can be applied to many things ranging from legitimate concerns for the safety of users or protection of property to perverse desires to conform uses to a social norm which is no less strict for being unwritten. (133)

129   Luc Leroux, "À Marseille, la SNCF reporte son projet d'équiper de néons bleus une gare pour éloigner les toxicomanes," *Le Monde,* November 24, 2012, https://www.lemonde.fr/sante/article/2012/11/24/a-marseille-la-sncf-reporte-son-projet-d-equiper-de-neons-bleus-une-gare-pour-eloigner-les-toxicomanes_1795460_1651302.html., accessed April 20, 2019.   130   Laura Hubert, "De la lumière bleue dans les toilettes: la nouvelle arme anti drogue aux Etats-Unis," Neon Mag, June 2018, https://www.neonmag.fr/la-lumiere-bleue-pour-diminuer-les-shoots-de-drogue-dans-les-toilettes-publiques-auxetats-unis-508618.html.   131   Gordan Savicic and Selena Savic, *Upleasant Design* (Rotterdam/Vienna/Lausanne: G.L.O.R.I.A, 2013)   132   Jean-Pierre Ferrand, "Un tour du monde de l''architecture défensive'," *Sociotopes,* https://sociotopes.home.blog/2020/08/06/un-tour-du-monde-de-l-architecture-defensive/, accessed February 4, 2022.   133   Ferrand, "Un tour du monde."

ROTOR

Seven Tales about Toilets

Renaud Haerlingen

On the one hand, Rotor is a Brussels-based research and design practice that emerged in 2005 from a shared interest in investigating the organization of the material environment. On the other hand, since around 2015, we created off Rotor Deconstruction as a cooperative company selling perfectly reusable materials reclaimed from demolition sites. This evolution came from the realization that the real estate sector discards huge quantities of materials that are not necessarily old or obsolete. Confronted with a lack of economic actors to tackle the issue, we decided to create a prototype for such a business entity. Today we have a warehouse, a workshop, a showroom and an online marketplace.

For some, Rotor is associated with the field of architecture, but in the current group of more than 25 people, only some have studied architecture. Our collaboration operates amongst very different profiles. It was probably more a generational concern about resources and preserving values against entropy that brought us together. This particularity has led us to take a multitude of roles and to operate in varied contexts.

Lobby

When Roberto Zancan told me that he was launching a seminar on toilets, he had just called a Swiss architect

and tried to invite him but they could not have a conversation because the architect stated that for him, toilets were not an architectural topic. Somehow, I could relate to the subject, but I did not know what to do with toilets as a central point.

For a recent meeting, I visited the office of a high-end creative company whose work I have known for a long time. When I entered the lobby, in the middle, there was an illuminated cube. Coming closer, I noticed that it contained a life size replica of a toilet. As I could immediately recognize the work of the Korean sculptor Do Ho Suh, I did understand that it was a remarkable statement, but at the same time, I was nonplussed by the display of a toilet in plain sight.

I shall not build an articulated point of view on this topic, but I can reveal how toilets have played a prominent role in a series of our works. Have they shaped attitudes or forged interrogations? Let me take you into a corporate office building, a mode and design center, a carnival factory, a book gallery, the Olympic headquarters, an Italian hospital, and through a refurbishment installation.

Meeting room antechamber

In 2015, we were called by a large real estate owner in Belgium to visit a corporate office building on the outskirts of Brussels. They were about to remodel some meeting rooms and a series of facilities, so we did an inventory and assessed which materials to reclaim. Two of the rooms we surveyed were the toilets. They were mostly white and well-maintained. The tapware looked contemporary and the urinals were the standard model seen everywhere. At the time, I felt confounded by the decision to demolish these toilets. Although we had seen it all before in the office world, I still struggled to think about the why. Anyhow, that was it.

We did our job, we reclaimed and distributed a collection of materials, but a few months later, I happened to go back to that building. Using the corridor and the doors that I knew, they had changed everything! They had changed the toilets but they had also included floor to ceiling mirrors. The partitioning had a wood-like finish and I understood that what had changed was the program. These toilets were on the ground floor, next to a series of meeting rooms, and it probably made sense to have a place where you could find a different atmosphere from in the atrium. Now they could act as an antechamber, and I could imagine myself in that place, preparing for something. They demolished things that were not obsolete, but I realized that they had a point in making something other than the basic toilet.

White architecture

For the Center for Mode And Design in Brussels design competition, we joined forces with the architecture firm V+. The announced budget was six million euro, which did not sound fancy considering the size of the plot, and although the brief called for a new building, its purpose implied somewhat of a spectacle. Instead of demolishing the three ordinary buildings on the site, we won with an argument to keep them and, through minimal

transformations, to make the MAD iconic by working on the material palette of its interior! We claimed that as a kind of museum, this institution is inclined to fall into the 'white box' paradigm, but from a 'Rotorian' perspective there is no such thing as an abstract white. The materialization of such an idea happens through all kinds of shades. White paint is different from white marble, and white rubber feels different from white fabrics. Our goal became to design a most extraordinary white box made of a rich display of white textures.

We enjoyed calling countless construction materials companies to ask for samples of their white products. This built up into a very beautiful collection of whites. But to develop this kind of project, we had chosen to collaborate with a technical consulting company, then it went into the hands of a general contractor through a public tendering process, and these partners, along with the time and budget constraints, seemed to resist our ambition to do many things.

For the toilets, we did careful studies, questioning the where and how to hang your bag or your jacket once in the cubicle, we considered changing the generic doorknobs with porcelain ones, we explored the lighting possibilities, etc. We ended up with a complete project built around exotic low-cost fluorescent tubes with flowery shapes, but… we never submitted those files. Because it was the toilet, we felt like the busy meetings had no time for them.

The only idea we could pass through the construction documentation process was a proposal for the tiling. We imagined using absolutely generic 10 by 10 cm or 15 by 15 cm white tiles, with the twist that many companies

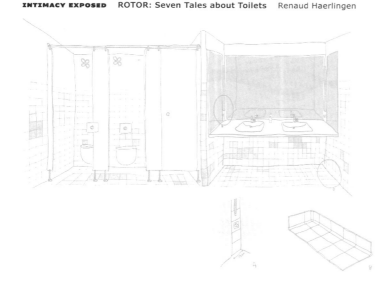

have their own basic white tile and they would slightly differ one from another. Our intention was that the contractor would buy several batches of white tiles from different producers and combine them randomly to build a texture with subtle variations. On site, the contractor purged the idea out of its curiosity for the manufacturing process, and they simply ordered three 'variations' of white from one catalog. Sadly, the result is poor! But because it was just the toilets, there was no room for argument.

Balancing the rough

In Brussels, the Zinneke Parade has been an institution since 2000. For many years its headquarters have been installed in temporary locations, but recently they moved to a site that they can renovate to suit their long-term needs. Zinneke's main public agenda is the organization of a big parade in the city once every two years, but this very special moment is mostly a pretext to foster social interactions in the neighborhoods along the way. For the parade itself, they need to build mobile structures, set up a metal workshop, and provide qualitative teaching. To develop other projects, they wanted to share the 2000 m² space they are responsible for as part of their willingness to support collective initiatives. The place is intentionally run on a low budget in order to facilitate broad inclusivity and ease the threshold for entering the place.

In such a context, a lot depends on people's willingness to tolerate the roughness of the situation and deal with the traces of others. If this is recognized and assumed, it could eventually limit the renovations and management expecta-

tions. But there have to be compromises most of the time, and we tried to push the argument that when you have to care for your own intimacy, it should be super-comfortable and over-deliver. This might reconcile one's relations with the otherwise non-pristine state of the building.

This renovation had been profiled as an exemplary project for the reuse of construction materials, so Rotor was intimately involved in the design. However, in our role as a specialist consultant, we did need to hire an architecture firm through a competition. We lost track of the jury designation process, and the job was given to a couple of young architects. Friendly, but possibly more concerned about their portfolio than curious for architecture and materiality.

From our side, we pushed for the showers and toilet spaces to be special and refined. In a playful tone, we suggested that the bathroom in the basement could eventually evolve into the typical Japanese common bath installation known as *Onsen*. It would be so much nicer than lockers and showers! The renovation project has a tight budget, but couldn't we choose to afford just that one? For the toilets, we proposed to articulate the space around a large handwashing fountain that we could find on the reuse market. Then we associated this idea with an exploration of the regulation for toilets with the hand washbasin included in a complete entity which would allow for the fountain room to be a mixed area. With such a layout, these toilets would turn into a kind of underground lobby connected to the courtyard.

For a while, we enjoyed having these perspectives in the plans, but when the architects took over, the idea of compensating for the roughness of the overall project was

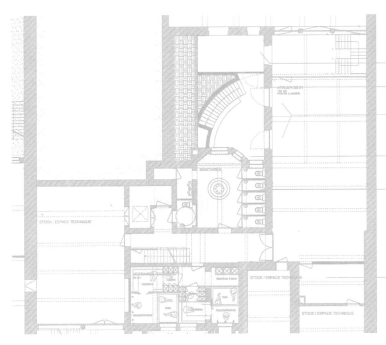

lost. My perception was that they accepted that for a low budget, their reference could be the showers at camping grounds, which is what it became, and the toilets turned out to be a corridor with a very conventional division.

In the end, we could only be the 'reuse consultant' and we presented the collection of reclaimed materials in a showroom to be integrated with the project. Of course, we reclaimed toilet bowls, so everybody seemed happy at the table, but all the same, I'm glad to report on the story of our motivations for reconsidering the bathroom.

Serving a book gallery

After spending many years working for European institutions in Brussels, Mr. Parodi came up with a project for a bookstore that would offer novels in every language used in the EU. To design the place with a sensitivity for the environmental footprint, he asked Rotor for support. His idea was also that the use of reclaimed furniture and materials would give the place an identity. We started by touring Rotor's warehouse and curated a collection of elements: cupboards from a laboratory, ceiling lamps from a bank canteen, shelves from an old library, an architectural false-ceiling in wood and a solid oak parquet. Then we made a furnished model of the space, but the shop had an irregular geometry and it didn't look good.

His radical idea was that the shop should feel like a gallery, with one big table to present 25 books in 25 languages. So, although he believed Rotor should only use pre-existing materials, we had the feeling that the project would be better if it felt more like a single space.

We argued for the construction of an open wall that would establish a secondary space. This would be an area to serve food and drink on special occasions, and it would carefully frame the entrance to the bathroom and the small kitchen. This in-between space became surprisingly important for us, and we found ourselves worrying over the details of the interior design. It had to have wallpaper, preferably blue!

We started the process of choosing the new material. We looked at catalogs, we asked for samples, but with only a few weeks before the store opened, we still hadn't received many replies and we felt like there were many more options than the ones we could consider. All in all, it was a rather frustrating process, but we eventually signed off for one reference with the client, and that was going to be it.

A few days later, we received an email from our colleague Benjamin Lasserre with the text, "It's a win!", along with a series of photos showing a strange setting with people wearing white clothes and pasting impressive wallpaper in a shop.

Benjamin is a scenographer and he followed through with a late-night idea of earlier days. He went to the Opera, and asked some technicians if they had any discarded backdrop paintings from a performance that could be used as wallpaper. The guys unfolded a spectacular scene, luckily quite blueish, and in exchange for bottles of champagne, he made a deal with them to come and install the painting on the wall. The result was beyond our expectations, and the toilets and services area became the prize feature of this project.

Olympic standards

When the International Olympic Committee decided to demolish their office building in Lausanne to build new and larger headquarters, they knew that as a public institution, they had to do the right thing. A *deconstruction task force* was set up ,and under the umbrella of an EPFL student workshop, we've been invited to assess the reuse potential.

The group of experts had designed an ambitious plan to sort the demolition waste properly and proceed with a large percentage of recycling, but they could not see materials being reused within their conception of the Swiss context. If anything, they mentioned the white marble cladding in the main hall. World leaders and important people had been here, and sometimes it was even engraved with rings in an allusion to the prestigious Olympic logo. Their second focus was the Salle Pierre de Coubertin, where Olympic decisions have been taken. This was an important room, so could the materials be somewhat precious?

Symbolism was uppermost in their minds, but we explained that the reuse perspective is more diverse and slightly more complex. It depends on the material's dismountability, a series of logistical steps and the identification of a potential demand. Most of the time, relevance cannot be judged on the basis of the appearance of things. It often requires hands-on testing and the results of this investigation are often counter-intuitive.

We tested dismantling the marble, and beneath its apparent unity there were three different attachment systems. On most of the surface, the stone had been glued directly to partition walls with an epoxy composite, and only in

some areas was it secured at a distance from the wall with metallic studs that we could cut. Also, we discovered from the original construction documents that it was Brazilian stone and not an exceptionally renowned marble.

We then entered the bathrooms and encountered a large series of cutely-shaped washbasins in very good state, branded with the name of a leading Swiss company. As expected, dismounting was smooth and they joined the collection of elements that proved to be reclaimable.

Parallel to this inventory, the students searched for 'demand' and made a list of actors potentially interested in these resources. One of them was Pro-Maison, a social enterprise based in Lausanne which regularly supplies plumbers with second-hand materials for social housing repairs. It was immediately agreed that they would take the collection of sanitary appliances. This marked a significant achievement for the *deconstruction task force*. A few months later, I visited their shop and was pleased to find the IOC wash basins for sale. They even had a significant market value, with a price tag of 180 CHF for the mid-sized items.

Toilet cisterns in Prato

The municipality of Prato in Italy called an international competition to turn the site of its old hospital into a large central park. It needed to demolish the existing building, and invited Rotor to join the project. We were commissioned to make an inventory of what could be reused and eventually think about the design of a small pavilion. So, we went there and did our survey.

In the hospital we discovered some funny elements like a collection of dismountable colored handrails, lots of different doors, cast iron radiators and some stone, but on the whole nothing very precious. It was a properly worn-out public building.

During this mission, we had a sudden crush on the old water cisterns for flushing the toilets! There were two models, both of them seductive. Although we still didn't know what their potential use could be, because this kind of system is mostly obsolete today, we included them in the sanitary equipment page of the document anyway, simply listed as "a very beautiful shape".

Re-circulating toilet bowls

As much as Rotor Deconstruction is a reclamation and trade business, it is also a research entity that allows us to explore the limits of what can possibly be reclaimed from pre-existing stocks. At the time of this invitation, we had received an invitation from *Vlaanderen Circulair* to explore the feasibility of reclaiming and refurbishing porcelain toilet bowls and urinals. Our goal was to set up an installation that could process an initial batch of about 100 items for a big project in Brussels.

We collected used bowls with traces of wear and tear, and the first thing we learned about them is that it's not so much the visible part of the object that is worrisome. Above all it is the astonishing calcium carbonate scales that form in the boxed rims and ducts of the bowls that need to be properly dissolved in order to justify an extended lifespan. This project was led by Daniel van Drimmelen,

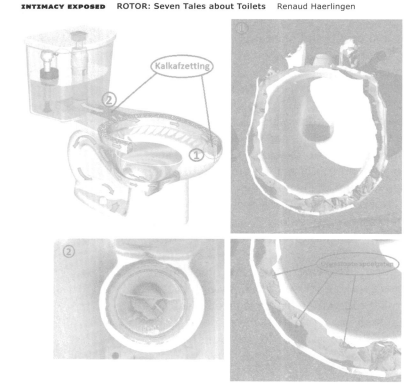

a colleague with a background in bio-engineering, who methodically tested the reactions of several soft acids on the limestone and the porcelain. He eventually settled for the relatively cheap *Strip-A-Way Powder* that is activated by pumping air bubbles into a bath. Beyond the laboratory exploration, to streamline the process, he set up a workshop with an overhead crane and standardized safety measures. Finally, the bath lifetime, additional cleaning and packaging issues were fine-tuned and we were able to supply the original order.

The results of the research have been published in a report, and we have reached an almost competitive price. Nevertheless, with generic low-cost bowls readily available, the current conclusion for Rotor is that it is still too expensive to refurbish toilets in this semi-artisan way.

DEVICES, SPACES, ACTIONS AND PLACES FOR BODY CARE
elii's (134) works through Toilets.

Eva Gil Lopesino

Intimacy Exposed. Toilet, Bathroom, Restroom could not be more relevant or current. Examples of this abound. At the Reinvented Toilet Expo in Beijing (China), the Bill and Melinda Gates Foundation made the worldwide presentation of part of the research they have been carrying out for seven years on the development of an "off the grid" or "off-grid" toilet that needs no water and is not connected to plumbing and sewer systems. (135) The toilet has even been shortlisted as one of the fifteen devices that, according to Rem Koolhaas and his *Fundamentals* exhibition for the 14th Venice Architecture Biennale (2014), have configured architecture since its very start. Indeed, growing interest in the subject can be found in academic circles such as the inaugural theme of *Room Journal*, (136) whose first issue was devoted to the concept of the bathroom and included articles by artists, writers, and architects. These are only a few of the examples that witness the growing interest in having this device included in the narrative of the history of architecture.

It was noted that the word toilet was of French origin and is used in much of the Western world to refer to public or private spaces where people expose their bodies to perform a variety of actions, from the most basic and functionalist for evacuating bodily fluids by urinating or defecating to other, more sophisticated but less immediate ones such

as putting on makeup, combing or brushing one's hair, talking on the phone, having a smoke, reading, hiding, having sex, taking drugs, pumping out breast milk, chatting or taking a daily break, murdering, chopping up the dead body, or even generating your own energy, as we will see in a few examples further on.

If we look at how the meaning of the word toilet has changed over time, it may help us come up with a classification of some of the works at elii that address their construction and thus better understand these technological devices, these places, usually indoors, called toilets, bathrooms, or restrooms, where the body and its care take the lead role. In fact, the original meaning of the word in the French dictionary in 1763 (137) described toilet as a small piece of cloth or canvas placed on top of a shelf along with other toiletries (i.e., objects for cleaning and being in contact with the body), a two-dimensional object, a plane, where the basic unit of measure was surface area (m^2s). Later, the word came to be used to designate a larger, three-dimensional object, a piece of furniture where the basic unit of measure was length (m) to give us the dimensions of the object (i.e., an object on which the body rests). It went on to refer to a separate, private three-dimensional volumetric place or room (138) where the basic unit of measure was volume (m^3) (i.e., a space that embraces and encloses the body and that is occupied by the body). What we know as the toilet today may be considered a setting, a complex atmosphere, a meeting place that crystallizes and materializes many of the contemporary concerns regarding architecture and its most intimate relationship with the bodies of those who inhabit it.

134   architecture office   135   See Bill and Melinda Gates Foundation, "Bill Gates Launches Reinvented Toilet Expo Showcasing New Pathogen-Killing Sanitation Products That Don't Require Sewers or Water Lines," November 6, 2018, https://www.gatesfoundation.org/Media-Center/Press-Releases/2018/11/Bill-Gates-Launches-Reinvented-Toilet-Expo-Showcasing-New-Pathogen-Killing-Sanitation-Products., accessed December 6, 2018.
136   See *Room Journal: The Bathroom* (Vancouver: University of British Columbia, 2019).   137   Formerly the *toilet* was simply a small canvas, as defined in *Dictionnaire universel françois et latin, vulgairement appelé Dictionnaire de Trévoux* (Paris: La Compagnie des Libraires Associés, 1762).
138   As mentioned in the poem *Don Juan*, by Lord Byron in 1819, the toilet was: "a private room for dressing later with a toilet bowl. [...] There is the closet, there the toilet" Lord Byron, *Don Juan*, (London: Thomas Davison, 1819–21), 79.

the word toilet mutated and enlarged its radius of action and effect, going from referring to a plane, then to an object, then to a room, and finally to a complex contemporary setting full of other things.

Another possible classification for us to arrange our ideas around what a toilet is for the work carried out at elii can be taken from the eleventh volume of *Elements of Architecture*, by OMA, already mentioned above, (139) in which the concept was included as one of the fifteen points of reference or elements that architecture deals with and that acts as a link between it and the clients as well as society.

The eleventh book of the collection associated with the exhibition, also called Toilet, and contained a reflection by the curator, Rem Koolhaas, on this element: never before had the bathroom, the restroom, the head, the WC or the toilet ever been included in an architectural treatise as a primordial element. (140) The text established a possible classification based on the evolution of the word toilet as a configuring element of architectures: first the toilet referred to an object (a complex technological device) ["the discrete device itself"], then it meant a room (a space or compartment) ["the room in which it is situated"] then ended up alluding to an action (a complex environment of relations and actions) ["the act of cleansing"]. (141)

We will use this classification proposed by Rem Koolhaas while also relying on the evolution of the term described by Zancan to list some of the work of our office regarding the toilet concept in order to better explain some of the proposals made by elii over the last ten years.

Writing this text, we were reminded of the words of the Spanish artist and designer César Manrique who affirmed that the bathroom was the only indispensable place in a dwelling. It was the room or place where you normally started the day and where you finished it, so the place had to be cozy and comfortable enough to be able to host a business meeting. For Manrique, the toilet had to be able to host a social and collective encounter, not only because of its physical dimensions but also because of the sophistication of its design and layout. The bathrooms of his architectural designs had large dimensions and exuded hedonism in their conception. According to Violeta Izquierdo, César Manrique did not conceive bathrooms as secondary places. instead he endowed them with artistic category, blurring the distinction between indoors and outdoors, between the intimate and the public, breaking those physical and visual limits. (142) These rooms are spaces for taking care of the body and relationships. Moreover, if, as the World Toilet Organization (WTO) states, we use the bathroom six to eight times a day (143) in Western culture, we should as designers reconsider this room as a primordial element in our daily lives and a device worthy of our devoting time and attention to its conception. In the work done by the office especially regarding domestic spaces, we have always tried to pay special attention to these devices, spaces and environments of body care, addressing its design with care.

139   Irma Boom et al., *Elements of Architecture: Toilet*, vol. 11 (Venice: Marsilio Editori, 2014).   140   See Boom et al., *Elements of Architecture: Toilet*, 1103. 141   Boom et al., *Elements of Architecture: Toilet*, 1103.   142   Violeta Izquierdo, *La obra artística de César Manrique*, (Madrid: Universidad Autónoma de Madrid, 1996).   143   See World Toilet Organization, *Advocacy Guideraising. A Stink for a World Toilet Day* (World Toilet Organization, 2015).

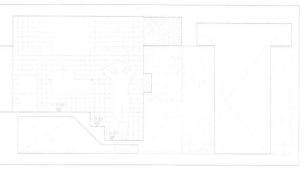

Toilet as an object/as a technological device

Some of the projects by elii develop on the idea that our day-to-day life is a kind of soap opera. Especially in domestic spaces, elii works on many projects with the idea that "each house is a theatre", comparing domestic space with a stage where architecture is its backdrop. People perform and rehearse their new lives in these spaces for the recreation of domestic fictions. In many of our projects, the spatial devices we occupy are designed as transformable stage settings designed for the choreography, rehearsal, action and fiction of our everyday lives. These objects are equipped to further intensify the performative experience of the bodies of their users, to test and question their social roles and the limits of the shared, to rehearse common imaginaries, to analyze their subjectivity and to explore the potential of the ordinary.

In the work *097-Yojigen Poketto* (literally, 'pocket of the fourth dimension', which is the name of the Japanese anime character Doraemon's pocket, the one from which he pulls out amazing items from the future) the toilet-object was configured to maximize the volume of the habitable space in the refurbishment of an early-20th century apartment in downtown Madrid. The entire toilet-device was raised 90 centimeters above the original floor level of the dwelling to allow 'extra' functions to be integrated into the domestic space, such as a bathtub deeper than the ones sold on the market, some of the plumbing and sewage installations, some of the storage of the home, etc., thereby optimizing every cubic meter of the house. Although the toilet-device is described by its basic units

of length measurements in meters (m), it is designed to maximize the volumetric conditions of the environment in which it is inscribed (m³). Furthermore, when the floor level of the device was raised, it put one of the original windows of the facade directly in line with the bathroom floor, letting natural light stream through the adjacent area for the toilet fixture (and perhaps bathing the bodies seated on it) and through the regular infinite white and red grid that covered every surface of the object, the floor and the walls of the device in an attempt to undo their physical limits to make the space larger while also making the built-in bathtub. With that same logic of dissolving the limits between the intimate and the more public and shared, as Manrique did, the partition dividing the toilet-object from the living room consists of a movable translucent and transparent sheet of glass to physically and visually relate both areas that lets the actions on both side of the plane be discerned and shared.

The refurbishment *106·Oki* of a residential unit in Madrid in the 1980s, the toilet-device was configured as an object enveloping the bodies of its occupants, using the curve as its basic geometry, as in the rest of the project, to build a seat in the shower area. The toilet-object, in this case meant to be enjoyed by only one person, rested on the curve that originated all the middle space of the room in the apartment, with all the other rooms articulated around it. The toilet-device came about as a result of the negotiation between the dimensions of the body it was to house

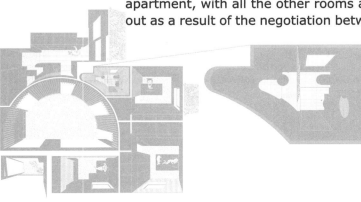

and the resulting geometry of the different pieces that fit together to complete the spatial scheme of the dwelling. The toilet-object became a space for introspection, for hiding behind a secret door darker in tone, also covered in a geometric grid meant to blur its true dimensions, making the toilet-object unfold along all its parameters. Strictly controlled lighting was added, designed with the client's own input. It included special light fixtures that could change the chromatic range of the light in the room and thereby transform and configure the domestic setting of the toilet-device at will, much like a stage (in this case, a theater designed for one single spectator/actor). In this case, the visual limits of the object are opaque and not related to the other rooms in the domestic space by the express wishes of the client. In contrast, its physical limits are the result of a negotiation among the various different object-devices that compose the dwelling, ones in which the laws of a circumference chord take on a leading role.

In project *067-Didomestic*, the toilet-object is decomposed and some of its elements, such as the bathtub-object or the dressing table-object, are set beside other room arrangements such as the living room or the bedroom. This refurbishment consisting of outfitting a domestic space on two levels (a main floor and its attic space) makes use of the edge of the newly built floor slab to include some toilet-objects, among

other elements, to configure an object equipped in a domestic space similar to that of the gridiron up in the heavens of a black-box stage, establishing a physical mimesis between the two worlds: the house and the theater. In the design, a toilet-device is placed on the more traditional ground floor, connected to the wet area of the dwelling. In addition, the bottom of a bathtub and a dressing table are set into the thickness of the new floor slab, as well as space to stow away some of the utensils associated with the toilet-object.

These objects were visually and physically connected, without any kind of vertical wall separating them, to other rooms of the house such as a small tea room and the master bedroom, squeezing the boundaries between what could be considered intimate and private and what could be considered more public and social within the domestic space. This is how they tried to equate these technological devices associated with the toilet-object with pieces and objects of furniture, as can be seen in this example of a living space in a residential unit in which the bathtub and the washbasin could be integrated into the living room as two more pieces or objects of furniture (objects on which the body rested), using the same materials for their construction and proposing a cozy, comfortable shared space within the social sphere associated with domestic spaces.

In *067-Didomestic*, inhabiting these objects belonging to the toilet-device, a meeting could be held, as Manrique stated, since its direct physical connection with other rooms would allow one to take a bath while other people were having tea in the sitting room or bedroom. All compartments and gates built into the floor and ceiling delimited by the thickness of the floor, as well as the bathtub, appeared and disappeared at the user's whim. Secret hatches, delicately padded and lined with the same soft fabric of baroque decorations and brocades as some of the movable walls of the dwelling, complemented the basic configuration of the living space according to the needs of the moment and enabled different domestic combinations to be arranged. These two objects were placed as just another element among the furniture of the house, decentralizing the toilet-object in a single place to disseminate it around all the rooms.

Toilet as space, room, and place

If we approach the toilet concept and focus our attention on its definition as an inhabited space, room or area, as a space that is already occupied and inhabited by the body, we could include elii's projects that try to stretch that which can be constituted as political matter. Firstly, by making the toilet-room a space that can blur various types of boundaries: between what is considered public and private and intimate, within the configuration of a traditional Western home. (144) In addition, the limit and compartmentalization between the public sphere and the private sphere in a

more urban context, underscoring the interscalar nature of the day-to-day behaviors where all our daily work unfolds (bringing the actions unfolded in domestic spaces to the controversies of a global nature; for example, the choice of the deodorant--and its components-- that you use in your everyday life can have consequences on the habitat of the panda bears in China). Between what is a space for the care of a single individual and the care of many in a collective action shared with others (for example, adopting as possible the dystopia shown by the filmmaker Luis Buñuel in his 1974 film *Le fantôme de la liberté*, in which various actions that unfold around the toilet device were part of the public and social sphere, and therefore shared with others, and the act of eating was part of a more private and individual sphere, more intimate, removed to a space separate from the places for socialization in the home).

Taking into consideration these ways of diluting the limits associated with the toilet-space, we may consider the toilet ultimately as both an urban element and a political element at the same time. With these premises is how the toilet-space was developed in the project *057-Insider* (2011), which operated with a strategy similar to Yojigen Poketto's, in which the floor of the toilet-space was raised 60 centimeters with respect to the original floor of the house to rehabilitate to hold a bathtub, the bed, the plumbing and sewer facilities and all bathroom fixtures as a toilet-object. The spaces devoted to body care were gathered together in the middle of the home to configure two interior facades whose composition and material emulated the existing ones in the nearby surroundings of the historical downtown of Zaragoza. The two facades showed and

144   For example, including bathroom fixtures as exclusive protagonists of the domestic space as Shigeru Ban did in his wall-less House in Nagano in 1997, where the toilets occupied a common space shared without any physical interior compartmentalization with the rest of the design patterns and rooms in the house. Shigeru Ban, *Wall-less House*, Nagano, Japan (1997).

shared the actions unfolding in the toilet-room with the living area. The actions of care associated with the toilet-space were socialized, they were included in the area most traditionally considered public in a dwelling: the living room or sitting room, aiming to eliminate the limits set between both spaces. The toilet-space escaped from the individual enclosed space where it was usually placed to form part of the imaginary and possibilities of shared rituals. Several windows fitted with blinds were used to show various uses associated with the toilet-room and transfer them to the main living space of the house, where a chat could be shared between someone who was taking a shower and someone who was cooking or sitting on a sofa (again Manrique and his meeting). The project attempted to blur the boundaries between the intimate and the public, proposing other ways of sharing time and being together (bringing the actions that might occur in this domestic space closer to those that occur, for example, in the Arabic hammam, in the Nordic sauna or in shared Asian baths.

These proposals aimed to show the ability of these devices to unfold spaces and domestic actions as potential places for politics and thus blur the distinction between public and private spaces to make the point that everyday behaviors can be integrated into other scales of action beyond the home. Or, the other way around, to catch a glimpse of "private" activities in larger-scale political projects. In this example, the physical and visual connection of several rooms of different natures is made more evident, allowing their customization over time, revealing or hiding parts of the toilet-room or other uses, at the whim of its occupants.

A similar but subtler attempt was also made to blur the boundary between different spheres in the 055·House of Would project. Here, the master toilet-room was visually connected to the master bedroom to bring more natural light into the latter by using the toilet-space as a light well and a translucent polycarbonate and opal white connector between the pieces of wood that make up the bedrooms. This physical connection through a sheet of transparent glass delved again into the idea of trying to blur and play with the limits between what belongs to the sphere of the intimate, such as the toilet-space, and what belongs to the more public sphere, of a more shared nature, such as the bedroom-space. The toilet-room arose from a negotiation between the geometry of the gradient of the plot where the single-family home was located and the dimensions and rules of play of the body and its different positions. The toilet-room was used as a physical connector between the different pieces of laminated wood located at different heights that housed the bedrooms, allowing the construction of a built-in bathtub-shower that acted as a junction piece between the two. The dimensions of the bathtub-shower itself fit the dimensions of the body, of the different positions that it could adopt when used as a shower (alone or in company), bathtub (alone or in company), recliner, footbath, children's bath, etc. as described in the Poliban patent. (145) This toilet-space was designed for the enjoyment and care of the bodies

145   See Justo García Navarro, *El Diseño de la higiene: origen y evolución histórica de los aparatos sanitarios* (Madrid: Fundación Cultural COAM, 2001), 65.

that would inhabit it. Furthermore, the colors that would make it up were chosen in close collaboration with the client, with a sea green tone for the joints of the gresite pieces that reminded the sunsets of the beaches of the world described by the artist Lydia de Koning in her work *Venice Beach* (2003).

Toilet as action

One of the examples that takes the toilet concept to the extreme is 069·JF·Kit House, a work that could fall under the classification of toilet as a verb or action: the act or action of washing (in the archaic sense), grooming and sprucing up one's appearance; or the action of using the toilet; of the help given to someone, especially to a child, to make use of it.

What would happen in a dystopian reality if some of the energy demands of the domestic spaces we normally inhabit in Western societies, one of which is the toilet, had to be powered by our bodies, our muscles and our day-to-day physical activities? What actions would we need to unfold in order to be able to flush the toilet or to take a hot bath? (146)

JF-Kit House BR and GZ explored the rhetorical and controversial dimension of architecture. Its objective was not so much to provide a closed solution, but to open a debate in society. It used architecture unfolded as a fictional setting in which the visitor could

wonder and try out other realities, turning the museum into a playground for critique, into a laboratory. The exhibition space became a space for experimentation.

If sustainability entails a cultural transformation, society as a whole must discuss how it wants that new culture to be. JF-Kit House participated in this debate by materializing a future possibility in an architectural prototype so that citizens could experience it, inhabit it and discuss its viability. It was an architectural political fiction that had to be debated and evaluated to try out how domestic space and its ritual uses would be transformed, as well as citizens' bodies in an "off the grid" context on account of the stance on sustainability.

This work was aimed at joining certain trends in the history of architecture that show proposals for the house of the future. (147) JF-Kit House BR and GZ sought to take a different stance, initiating a dialogue rather than closing a conversation. It proposed a space to inhabit controversy: not a spatial solution as a final state but as a starting point. Thinking of any scenario that addresses the energy question inevitably entails reinventing a new culture, and at this point, the body is a leading actor in the story. In this 1:1 scale prototype, like the one by Jacobsen and the Smithsons, bodies would become transformed and modified by the daily physical action that they would have to undertake when carrying out the most common daily activities in the rooms of the house. This is how JF-Kit House revealed the body as a critical transit point and a key battlefield in the articulation of sustainable futures. By taking the centrality of the body to the extreme, the house offered an ironic model of citizenship for future sustainable

146   The JF·Kit House (ELII, 2012) is an experimental prototype of a residential unit designed for two museum spaces: CIVA (Centre International pour la Ville, l'Architecture et le Paysage) in Brussels (BR) and Guangdong Museum of Art in Guangzhou (GZ). Its name plays on the initials of the actress and political activist Jane Fonda who through her workout videos was able to transform the living rooms of thousands of viewers into gyms to tone their bodies.
147   The prototype produced by Arne Jacobsen and Flemming Lassen for the competition promoted by the Danish Association of Architects in 1929 (see Félix Solaguren, *Arne Jacobsen: Edificios públicos: Public Buildings* (Barcelona: Editorial Gustavo Gili, 2005)), the one developed by the architects Alison and Peter Smithson for the exhibition *Daily Mail Ideal Home* in 1956 called House of the Future (see Sabine von Fischer, "The Sound of the Future," Canadian Centre for Architecture, 2010, www.cca.qc.ca/en/issues/2/what-the-future-looked-like/32734/1956-house-of-the-future), or the proposal by the architect Andreis Legzdins for the Swiss Electronic Fair in 1973 showing a prototype of domestic space for the foreseeable future in 1997 (see Justo García Navarro, *El cuarto de baño en la vivienda urbana: una perspectiva histórica* (Madrid: Fundación Cultural COAM, 1998), 162) are several examples of this narrative. Both prototypes were at a 1:1 scale and attempted to anticipate solutions for the domestic space, including the toilet room and the toilet as an object in itself, offering utopian and normative solutions, putting an end to a possible conversation on the topic at hand, accessed April 10, 2019.

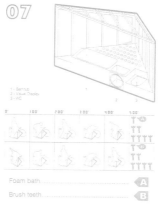

1 - Bathtub
2 - Visual Display
3 - WC

Foam bath .... A
Brush teeth .... B

societies: the "Jane Fonda Citizenship Model," which defined the ideal citizen as an individual who could meet all of his or her household energy needs through his or her own physical exercise. By radicalizing this model, JF-Kit House sought to open a debate on the type of bodies required for political participation and for the proper functioning of economically sustainable systems. Specifically, JF-Kit House asked us: What types of bodies are imagined to fulfill the promises of these sustainable futures? What kind of domestic infrastructure is required to produce these bodies? What are the new rituals, practices and domestic habits that these bodies will have to inscribe and promulgate? And most importantly: which organisms are excluded from participating in these sustainable futures and their pledges?

For example, many bodies would find themselves excluded from these domestic spaces, such as all the bodies belonging to people with different capabilities, or the bodies of the elderly or of babies.

If we take Rem Koolhaas's statement in his text *A Room of One's Own* in which he quotes: "A toilet is the fundamental zone of interaction - on the most intimate level - between humans and architecture" (148) we can affirm that in the toilet of the JF-Kit House, prominence of the body is intensified, taking on a triple role. Firstly, as a place of fundamental interaction with architecture, particularly in that specific domestic space (the body comes into more direct contact with architecture, with no filters). Secondly, recognizing the body as the object of measurement and design (149) for this particular

INTIMACY EXPOSED Devices, spaces, actions and places for body care elii's works through Toilets. Eva Gil Lopesino

100

space, given that most of its elements are designed based on ergonomic studies that attempt to accommodate and adapt to the shapes and dimensions of the different bodies they are meant to house. And thirdly, specifically, having the bodies be responsible for generating the energy that make it possible for all the actions to take place there. It is in the example of the JF-kit House that the toilet as an action (to toilet: action of assisting or supervising someone, especially an infant or invalid, in using a toilet) gains relevance in the work of the study. It is the place where the toilet ritual is turned into action through the movement and physical exercises of the bodies that inhabit it (assisting that of others or that of oneself), maximizing its role in the domestic architectural space. Thus, the space of the toilet in this prototype would no longer be just an infrastructure terminal where an intricate network of pipes ends connecting this domestic space with a larger, territorial-scale reality (it links our toilets to the reservoirs that supply our homes with water, and our sewers with the rivers and seas). It would not only be a space that receives the supply of water and energy, but would also become a productive space for a portion of these elements.

The toilet space would not only be a space in which to take a hot water bubble bath but also the energy-producing space to pump that water to the tub and heat it up to the desired temperature. It would be a space in which action is the protagonist even

148 Koolhaas, Rem, *A Room of One's Own, Elements of Architecture*: Toilet, (Venice: Marsilio Editori, 2014), 1003. 149 See Alexander Kira, *The Bathroom: Criteria for Design* (New York: Cornell University, 1966), 126–127, with all the detailed ergonomic studies of bodies of different sexes so as to redesign the toilet.

before the main action of bathing is perforated. That ritual, sometimes individual, that makes up a small daily luxury would be modified and implemented, perhaps giving way to new social rituals with an audience of more than one body. (150)

Thus, in the Body Recovery 07 space, a series of equivalences were indicated to be able to enjoy small experiences in the bathroom such as brushing one's teeth or taking a bath. For the latter, an inhabitant of the prototype would need to pedal for more than 450' (more than 7 hours) to be able to take a restorative bath or perhaps establish a new tradition in which the bubble bath would always be preceded by a shared spinning class with three other people (members of the same family or not) thereby shortening the workout session to slightly over 110 minutes of group exercise. In these cases, the toilet space would become a collective place, closer to the images shown in Buñuel's film of which we spoke at the beginning of the article, rather than a place meant for individuality. (151)

Perhaps in the case of the JF-Kit House, the toilet space became more of a family room of shared actions due to the need to produce more energy or the desire to blur the boundaries between these spaces and the spaces for socializing, bringing the configuration of the prototype toilet closer to that of the shared Far Eastern, Arab or Nordic bathrooms where many of the actions that unfold there are carried out surrounded by other bodies, in public.

The JF-Kit House envisioned a future in which the private and intimate space of the home would be transformed into a place where it would be possible to engage in more

ambitious political projects, such as sustainable societies or low-carbon economies, through seemingly mundane choices and practices. It did so by showing, for example, how common household devices, such as "home exercise furniture", could be used productively to raise awareness of the energy and economic costs involved in everyday activities and in doing so, inducing other forms of consumption and political behavior.

150   The project was accompanied by a dossier, "Domestic Fitness Furniture," which showed some workouts associated with the domestic spaces making up the JF·Kit House and where the equivalences were given between the energy needed, for example, to take a hot bath and the amount of exercise to be done prior to that action by one person, two or four, through spinning sessions.   151   It could come close to the space described in the 1930s announcement of the American bathroom fixture brand Kohler of Kohler that asked: "Is your bathroom a family room?" but in a different sense (the ad advocated the inclusion of extra bathrooms in the homes of American families in order to escape from just such a family space that had to be shared between different members of a family at the beginning of the 20th century in order to enjoy those rooms alone). See See Boom et al., *Elements of Architecture: Toilet*, 1103.

"Lean over the bowl and then take a dive.
All of you are dead. I am alive."

—Philip K. Dick, *Ubik*, 1969 (152)

This final essay is not intended to be a conclusion to the volume, but rather a sort of examination of the research presented here and their consequences. It is a Verifica Incerta, an "uncertain verification", like the famous 1964 movie by Italian artists Gianfranco Baruchello and Alberto Griffi, screened for the first time at La Cinémathèque Française in May 1965 and presented by Marcel Duchamp, to whom it was dedicated. (153) A montage of reflections, a fragmented speculation, inspired by all the previous texts, which strives to reflect on these texts and declare what is missing, what has not been possible to include in the limited space and time of this book's production.

Following this spirit, the best way to begin this verification is perhaps to quote a couple of sentences from *Ubik*. (154) In his radical, controversial novel, Philip K. Dick declares that the bowl, the toilet bowl, is the edge of the interface between reality and imagination. Only by putting his head in the urinal (155) can the protagonists of the novel (and us) understand where the truth lies, what is the real world and what is the projection of our brain imagination. With such a clear/dirty statement, Dick graphically explains how, regardless of whether we are alive or dead, believers or non-believers, through the hole that confronts us every day when we open the toilet bowl, we realize that

152   Philip K. Dick, *Ubik*, (New York: Doubleday, 1969), 76   153   For the history and the meaning of this liminal film, see Umberto Eco, *Postille al Nome della rosa* (Milano: Bompiani, 1983).   154   Philip K. Dick, *Ubik* (New York: Doubleday, 1969). For the interpretation of this book, see Philip K. Dick's biography by Emmanuel Carrère, *Je suis vivant et vous êtes morts* (Paris: Le Seuil, 1993).   155   In the book, two different graffiti are evoked: one with the toilet and the other with the urinal.

there is a hidden universe outside of us; a universe that makes our daily lives possible and comfortable and at the same time reminds us of the traces of our darkest ancestral anxieties.

This aspect is highlighted in one section of Josiane Imhasly and Beka & Lemoine's exhibition: the projection of the famous *Trainspotting* sequence in which Ewan McGregor—who later became a Jedi thanks to this scene-plunges into the most putrid latrine of Edinburgh. We have an outside and we have an inside, and on the bowl, we expose our (invisible) interior and we look at our (psychological) interior. (156) Following the trail of what our body expels, entering the universe beyond the hole, can mean descending into the things that progress has hidden from us in the sewers of our big cities, in the subterranean Paris of *Le Miserables*, in the parallel Vienna of *The Third Man*… With modernity, what was predicted in the collective latrines of the ancient Romans has become a universal condition, even in space stations. Before inventing the holes scraped in the ground, humans were still animals that defecated or urinated on the ground. Everything was on display. Jerries and chamber pots did not change the condition. But the invention of the U-tube to avoid odors and the connection to the sewer system gave rise to a parallel universe that now stares at us. Aren't snakes and reptiles crawling out of the bowl one of the most distressing suburban nightmares? But since 1917, a bowl (or at least a urinal) has ceased to be a bowl…

156　Jean-Luc Nancy, "On the soul" in *Corpus* (New York: Fordaham University Press, 2008). This lecture was given on April 8, 1994, at the Regional School of the Fine Arts in Le Mans, after a colloquium on The Body. The text was previously published in the acts of the colloquium, *The Weight of the Body* (Le Mans: Beaux-Arts, 1995).

Close/Open that door!

"Does architecture interest you? Not at all!"　　　　—Marcel Duchamp, interview by Michel Sanouillet, 1954

As might be expected, several essays in this book discuss *Fountain*. They focus on the attribution of the work of art and its crucial role in making the bathroom an instrument of artistic and social criticism. Nevertheless, there is another Duchamp project involving the bathroom: *Door, 11 rue Larrey*. Its relevance in the context of this volume is crucial. Not only because it is connected to a space dedicated to cleaning and washing the body, but precisely because it is undoubtedly attributable to the French artist. The more historians tend not to attribute the overthrow of the urinoir to Duchamp, the more this door increases in relevance for evaluating the surrealist work on the bathroom. Not only that, *Door, 11 rue Larrey* is in fact an element of a larger architectural project. In other words, it is the only architecture that the French artist designed and was built on the basis of his indications.

In general, analyses of this work have focused on the dialectic between language games and domestic objects. (157) They celebrate and discuss an oxymoron, the irony of the realization of an apparently impossible condition, that of a door both closed and open which, as Duchamp himself says, "caught the French proverb 'A door must be either

157　Bernhard Siegert and John Durham Peters, "Doors: On the Materiality of the Symbolic," *Grey Room* no. 47 (Cambridge: MIT Press, 2012), 6–23.

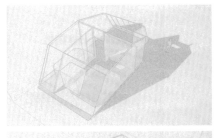

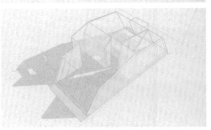

opened or closed' in fragante delicto for its inexactitude". However, there is perhaps no more functionalist episode in Duchamp's career than this. Although the exact sequence of actions and choices in the renovation of his tiny studio remains unclear in all the reconstructions published to date, the work of art is designed to allow a more reserved use of the bathroom for the artist's young bride in their home/studio.

"Il n'y a pas de solution parce qu'il n'y a pas de probleme" (There is no solution because there is no problem), as Duchamp used to say.

The renovation involved the entire transformation of the small apartment including the creation of a bathroom before the couple became engaged, and then the construction of the door as an act of modification, completion, addition and adaptation. The solution is anything but anarchic or dysfunctional. It is not a "Bachelor Machine". On the contrary, we are looking at a perfectly functional space (the small recess for the bathtub), resolved with a concise and effective proposal, and then adapted to the needs of a "married couple". As the artist himself states explicitly (158), it is the person who visits or listens to the description of this home/studio, substantially devoid of the artist's works, which leads to the interpretation of the renovation as a Dadaist type of intervention.

If the urinoir is an extraction, the door is an insertion. This door was extracted only at the end of its functional life when, in the 1960s, the artist recovered it to raise its profile at international exhibitions. Duchamp transformed an

158   "In Paris I was living in a very tiny apartment. To take full advantage of the meager space, I thought to make use of a single door which would close alternatively on two jamb-linings placed at right angles. I showed it to some friends and commented that the proverb 'A door must be either open or closed' was thus caught in flagrante delicto for its inexactitude. But people have forgotten the practical reason that dictated the necessity of this measure and they only think of it as a Dada provocation." Marcel Duchamp, edited by Serge Stauffer, "Interview mit Michel Sanouillet (1954)," *Marcel Duchamp: Interviews und Statements* (Stuttgart: Hatje Cantz Publishers, 1992), 50.

architectural object into a gallery object, not so different from those that Gordon, the son of his friend Matta, soon produced in New York: a reuse quite similar to the one described in a chapter of this book, Rotor-Decostruction. Although some aspects of the project still remain obscure, the biography of Lydie Sarazin-Levassor is an effective verification of the many surrealist mythologies built up around *Door, 11 rue Larrey*, starting with the first "publication" of the work of art in the magazine *Orbes* in 1933, and then in *Médium* in 1953. (159)

"He had scraped away at the walls to get to the bare plaster and fitted a folding screen made of thin strips of wood by the front door to cut off any undesired visitors form the rest of the room. It was north-facing studio with a typically large window-space. A smaller window gave onto the roof to the south, and Marcel had fitted the bathroom on that side, having had to raise the floor by two or three steps in order to permit the water to drain, as our outlet pipe led straight onto the roof and into the gutter..." (160).

Mis à nu par sa mariée, Duchamp becomes... architect. The lifting of the floor, the drainage into the gutter and the other solutions speak of a non-overturning functionalism, an inventiveness that always opens up new possibilities, pushes for innovation, to obtain more useful and comfortable conditions from the existing technical order. The image of this door as something "always open" expresses better than any other surrealist invention the quality of the bathroom: a space of technological concentration which highlights social codes... to which Duchamp had to adapt

159   In 1933, Jean van Heeckeren and Jacques-Henry Lévesque commented on "La porte de Duchamp" for the first time in the Parisian review *Orbes*. "When you open this door, to go into the bedroom, it closes the entrance to the bathroom, and when you open this door to go into the bathroom, it closes the door to the studio..." "Il faut qu'une porte soit ouverte ou fermée" seems an irreducible truth. Nonetheless Marcel Duchamp has found a way to construct a door that is open and closed at the same time." Jean van Heeckeren and Jacques-Henry Lévesque, "La porte de Duchamp," *Orbes 2*, no. 2 (Paris: Summer 1933): XIV. An extract from the journal *Orbes*, was published in the magazine *Médium: Communication surréaliste, Nouvelle série* no. 1 (Paris: Editions Aroanes, 1953), 11–12, with a new diagram illustrating the door mechanism. In a conversation with Pierre Cabanne, Duchamp reports on the fate of the door. In 1963, Duchamp purchased the door from his landlady for about $20 and shipped it to the United States, where it became part of the Mary Sisler collection. See Pierre Cabanne, *Dialogues with Marcel Duchamp* (London: Thames and Hudson, 1979), 78. Since then the "Porte de Duchamp" has been a work of art. In 1965, it was displayed

himself, adding a door to allow his young wife's privacy. For these and many other reasons, the bathroom—much more than any other room in the house—is a space of subversion and progress (in a positive sense, which we wish to support here) for contemporary design as a solution to human problems.

Toilet: A Love Story

"Until the problem doesn't get personal,
no one's willing to fight find a solution."   —Narayan ("Naru") Sharma, *Toilet: A Love Story*, 2017 (161)

Some of the essays in this book that reflect on *Fountain* have described dialogue and gender conflicts. A re-reading of *Echec matrimoniale* (the original title of Lydie Sarazin-Levassor autobiography) between Marcel Duchamp and Lydie Sarazin-Levassor would be useful to understand this theme better. Therefore, it seems necessary to take up the theme of the bathroom as a place of dialogue / conflict of conjugal coexistence on the horizon of social progress in low and middle-income countries. For this purpose we are helped by a splendid film released just as we were organizing the seminar: *Toilet: Ek Prem Katha* (*Toilet: A Love Story*), a sarcastic Bollywood comedy co-produced, among others, by the protagonist and great Indian movie star, Akshay Kumar. (162)

in New York as part of the exhibition *Not Seen and/or Less Seen of/ by Marcel Duchamp/Rrose Sélavy*, 1904–1964. Under the heading of *Door: 11, rue Larrey*, it was entered as no. 426 in the catalog of Duchamp's works. See Arturo Schwartz, *The Complete Works of Marcel Duchamp*, vol. 2 (New York: Delano Greenbridge Editions, 1997), 717. Number 507 in the *Critical Catalogue Raisonné* is a reproduction of a drawing by Duchamp of the door. Schwartz, *The Complete Works of Marcel Duchamp*, 778.   160   Lydie Fischer Sarazin-Levassor, *Un échec matrimonial: Le coeur de la mariée mis à nu par son célibataire même*, (Dijon: Les Presses du réel, 2004), 67–68.   161   *Toilet: A Love Story* (original Title: *Toilet: Ek Prem Katha*) is a Indian Hindi-language film of 2017. Directed by Shree Narayan Singh, co-produced by Neeraj Pandey and Akshay Kumar, this comedy-drama stars Bhumi Pednekar and Akshay Kumar.

The movie is based on real facts and tells the story of Jaya (Bhumi Pednekar), an educated girl who goes to college and marries Keshav Sharma (Akshay Kumar), a man from another village, and moves in with his family, as is customary. The first morning after their marriage, she learns that her husband's family does not have a toilet in the house. The only way she can relieve herself is to join the village women, who get up every day at 4 am to defecate in the fields while it is still dark (for privacy reasons). And then they wait for sunset to use the fields again. She is horrified but the villagers, including her in-laws, firmly believe that having a toilet in the home, where there's a kitchen and a prayer room, is unclean. Keshav makes a couple of temporary adjustments to fix the problem. First, he takes Jaya to a neighbor's house which has a portable toilet for a bedridden elderly woman, and then to a train that has a seven-minute stop at the village railway station, but one day she is locked up in the toilet and the train leaves the station. After arguing with her husband and giving him an ultimatum - no bathroom, no wedding - she decides she has no choice but to leave the man she loves and returns to her parents' house. But Keshav sets out to win her back. And that means changing his mind about the need for sanitation. Not only that, she also plans to change the community's toilet position as well. The plot is quite complex and Keshav's attempts mostly clash with the reluctance of his father to acknowledge the importance of having a toilet in the house. Keshav starts to build a toilet, but the father arranges to demolish it while Keshav is asleep. The man, a very religious and superstitious priest, only realizes the

162   Shree Narayan Signh, directors, *Toilet: Ek Prem Katha* (Viacom 18 Motion Pictures et al., 2017)

problem one day when his old mother falls on the threshold and injures her hip as she is going out to defecate. She shouts vehemently that she absolutely cannot walk to defecate in the fields and that she must use the bathroom which, in the meantime, Keshav has re-built in the courtyard.

At this point, the interminable delays and complexity of the state bureaucracy replace the father's opposition and the solution seems impossible. Jaya files for divorce at a local court citing the unavailability of a bathroom in her husband's home as the main reason. Although the case receives a lot of media attention and politicians and concerned government departments act to speed up the construction of toilets in Keshav village, nothing changes… until the Chief Minister's officer suspends the right to go to the toilet during working hours for all public employees of the relevant offices until they solve the problem. Then Keshav's brother, Naru, declares the moral of the film: "The file which went nowhere in 12 months, got sanctioned in 12 minutes. That's when these officers learned their lesson… Until the problem gets personal, no-one is willing to fight for a solution." The story thus has a happy ending, Keshav and Jaya return to live together and in the final credits, women and men are seen lining up to use mobile toilets at the edge of the village while the construction of permanent toilets goes ahead.

A week after the film's release, Indian courts granted a divorce to a young woman on the grounds that her husband hadn't installed a toilet in their home, causing her much agony during their two-year marriage. Before the end

credits, the movie mentions that it is based on the story of a woman from Madhya Pradesh who refused to return to her husband's home because he did not have a bathroom. The story shares some similarities with an actual event in which 19-year-old fled her husband's home in 2012 when there was no bathroom. In addition, the director Praveen Vyas sent a legal notice to the producers claiming that the film plagiarized scenes and dialogues from his documentary Manini—financed by the Ministry of Information & Broadcasting—based on the same topic. Whatever the case, the truth is that it is the sarcastic comedy tone that makes Toilet: A love Story particularly effective and convincing to highlight India's open defecation problem.

Because of poverty and cultural and religious prejudices in rural areas, people still do not have this basic service. There are strong gender impacts related to outdoor defecation. The lack of safe private toilets makes women vulnerable to violence. Women are at risk of sexual harassment and rape as they search for places for defecation in the open where they can be secluded and private, often in the dark. Reports of assault in or near areas where women openly defecate are common. Lack of privacy has a particularly broad effect on their sense of dignity. They face the shame of having to defecate in public so often that they wait until sunset to free themselves, when the risk being attacked after dark is even greater.

The film is a comic drama about Prime Minister Narendra Modi's Swachh Bharat Abhiyan (Clean India Mission), a legislative battle to improve India's sanitation conditions, with a focus on diminishing defecation in the open in broad daylight, particularly in provincial India. Akshay Kumar dug a toilet in Madhya Pradesh to promote the film, and in an interview declared that if open defecation in India stopped, 30% of rapes would not happen because this 30% happens when women go into the field to relive themselves. (163)

Since the inception of the Swachh Bharat Abhiyan, rural sanitation in India has increased significantly from 39% in October 2014 to over 92% at the end of August 2018. Prime Minister Narendra Modi himself called the movie a very good effort to promote the program's message, and even Bill Gates,—whose Foundation shared with his ex-wife is engaged in a sanitary improvement program through toilets—listed the film as one of six good things that happened in 2017. (164)

Despite these tributes, the film has remained virtually unknown in Western countries, but has been a huge success throughout Asia. When it was released in China, it beat competition by the Disney production *Marvel Avengers: Infinity War* and other Hollywood blockbusters. In fact, the self-censorship structure of the Indian movie industry, which avoids gory scenes and topics, makes it particularly effective for programming in poorly democratic Asian and Islamic countries in general, where similar sanitization programs are underway such as the Go Wash program

163   Joginder Tuteja, "Exclusive Akshay Kumar Interview—I Am Doing All I Can to Make Sure That Toilet—Ek Prem Katha Is Seen by One and All," *Desimartini*, https://www.desimartini.com/news/martini-shots/archive/akshay-kumar-interview-toilet-ek-prem-katha-here-is-what-akshay-wanted-to-name-the-movie-article59388.htm accessed November 17, 2017.   164   Neetu Chandra Sharma, "Gates Foundation award seen as boost to Swachh Bharat Abhiyan," *LiveMint*, https://www.livemint.com/news/india/gates-foundation-award-seen-as-boost-to-swachh-bharat-abhiyan-1569432677658.html, accessed September 25, 2019.

in Bangladesh or Fresh Life in Africa. In other words, sometimes it is not necessary to be iconoclastic to achieve extensive success in the field of social promotion and women's emancipation. All you need is to engage directly with the problem-solving process. (165)

Le propre et le sale in details

"I do not like ducts, I do not like pipes. I hate them really thoroughly, but because I hate them so thoroughly, I feel that they have to be given their place. If I just hated them and took no care, I think that they would invade the building and completely destroy it."
                                                                                                                    —Louis Kahn (166)

As the essays by Eva Gil and Joel Sanders shows, practiced and built architecture can be useful in helping and discussing the social issues related to bathroom and toilets. Over the course of history, architects and artists connected to architecture have not only proposed projects but have often been aware that the evacuation issue could allow them to question their activity and the professional dimension of the discipline.

165   With regard to the difficulty of considering the toilet and its elements as "cultural objects," it is important to mention here the destruction of Branislav Nikolić's sculpture Endless Column, created for the Survive Work exhibition in Čačak, Serbia in December 2019. It was a 5-meter-tall sculpture composed of 11 ceramic toilet bowls in the shape of a pillar that juts into the sky, whose declared references were Brancusi and Duchamp. The intention of the artwork was not provocative. The artist did not want to scandalize with a brutal or ironic intervention. Instead, he wanted to create an object that produced plastic and aesthetic qualities through the reuse of everyday objects trouvé. Nevertheless, it provoked many reactions as soon as it was opened, and one night it was destroyed by unknown agents. The paradox is that the selection of the artist for the realization of this work was made on the basis of the Audience Award of the 27th Nadežda Petrović Memorial, which was approved by 10% of the population, a large number for a small town like Čačak.   166   Louis Kahn, quoted in *World Architecture I*, London, 1964, 35.

In the visual arts, the illustration of the bathroom is larger and more crucial than we think. Two outstanding examples come to mind: Francis Bacon's dazzling *The Black Triptycs* and *The Women's Bath* and *The Men's Bath* woodcuts by Albrecht Dürer. This helps us to realize that the tradition of architectural drawing of baths and toilets is as vast as it is little studied. (167) The first figure that comes to mind is the master of the art of engraving, Giambattista Piranesi, who proved that bathrooms, toilets, sewers and human evacuation could be use to magnify and also to reduce the importance of architecture. Amongst his immense output we can find detailed studies in sections, plans and technical diagrams of the Cloaca Maxima in *Della magnificenza ed architettura de' Romani*, and the frequent repetition of small characters intent on pissing on the ruins of some of the most important monuments of the Eternal City (such as the famous of Veduta della Basilica e di Piazza San Pietro, published in Vedute di Roma).

In this volume there is little space for illustrations and discussions of the technical drawings. Nevertheless, we believe that it is important to briefly mention this universe and how useful the study of its critical contribution could be, with at least two examples of the intriguing images that we found during our background research for this book. The first one is a plate in a series of drawings held at the Bibliotheque Nationale of Paris, showing the interior of a palace in Paris. The interiors depicted in the drawings are part of a project for Hôtel de Montholon (the building is at 23, Boulevard Poissonnière, previously Boulevard Montmartre), a commission given to François Soufflot le

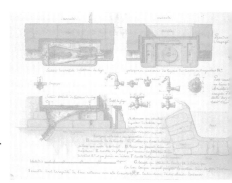

167   The purpose of this book is not to make the iconography of the bathroom and toilet theme in art, but it nevertheless seems appropriate to point out that this theme inevitably involves interior design. One of countless examples illustrates this aspect: the emblematic (self) portrait of Lee Miller in the bathtub at Adolf Hitler's apartment in Munich. Numerous essays have been written about this image, but no one seems to have noticed that the bathroom designed by Gerdy Troost is aligned on Prinzregentenstrasse, a few steps away from the Hofatelier Elvira, the famous photography studio design by August Endell, the first husband of Elsa von Freytag-Loringhoven, "the Dadaist Baroness" who probably invented *Fountain*. Elsa von Freytag-Loringhoven and Lee Miller never met, but they certainly would have had a lot to tell each other about the subversion of gender roles in the 20th century, in the realm of… the toilet.

Romain (nephew of the builder of the Pantheon) and executed by Jean Jacques Lequeu for wealthy magistrate and later president of the Parlement of Normandy, Nicolas de Montholon. The ineffable Lequeu used pen and wash to draw a colorful Plan des lieux à soupape (the name used for the toilet at the time in France, deriving from the valve that activated the drain mechanism). The plate features two plans and two cross-sections of the toilet, numerous details of the taps and a series of texts describing how the different elements work. In the horizontal and vertical "sections of the interior of the seat", ink and wash are used for a detailed description of the feces and swirls of water as the matter is impelled towards the pipe and the bottom plane is cleaned. This is probably the most detailed and "artistic" illustration of a toilet that exists, or at least that has remained. If Le Corbusier had known about these drawings, he probably would not have complained about the luck of Ledoux in not having to cope with piping, and presumably not even Kahn would have come to dislike so intensely the pipes that inspired him for the Richards Memorial Laboratories. (168)

Looking at more recent times, we would like to mention a series of figures produced by Bethold Lubetkin and Tecton Group for the Highpoint One in London, one of the first iconic modernist building in England. These drawings were probably by Gordon Cullen, who at the time was working in Lubetkin's office. One of figures is dedicated to the bathroom and explains that, "most of the fittings were specially made for the job, not for snobbish reasons but

168   Reyner Banham, *The Architecture of the Well-Tempered Environment* (London: The Architectural Press, 1969), 249.

due to the helplessness of manufacturers who ignore simple solutions for standard products". (169) Sketches and details compare the solutions attempted in Highpoint One for toilet paper holders, toilet bowls, washbasins and taps to standard ones. The captions illustrating the drawings indicate that smooth and rounded profiles, surfaces protected from water, hidden pipes and adjustable elements are more ration because they are "easy to clean". In the case of this wealthy residence in West London, the insistence on cleanliness comes not only from the hygienic vision of the 1930s, but from a "participatory approach", which does not resolve architecture into a simple aesthetic fact. Cleaning the interior furnishings is a daily activity that must be considered as much as the function.

"Forms follows… dirt and cleaning", Lequeu et Lubetkin-Cullen would say. (170) However, Highpoint One's images remind us of the most serious gap in this research, the discussion of the conditions of bathroom attendants and cleaners in relation to architecture. This gap has recently been addressed by several film-based denunciations and committed artistic reflections such as the documentaries by Polish film-maker Pawel Lozinski and *Maid in America* by Anayansi Prado (2004), and the fictional movies *Dirt* directed by Nancy Savoca (2003). (171) If this is an ethically terrible gap in our work, it nevertheless helps us to realize just how much remains to be studied in the realm of the research issue which we wish to promote with this book.

169   John Allan, *Berthold Lubetkin: Architecture and the tradition of progress* (London: RIBA Publications, 1992), 199–201. The RIBA Drawing collection also includes a series of sketches related to this project for an exhibition panel illustrating the problems and solutions connected with designing for the elderly (a man shown lowering himself into a bath, a couple unable to operate a complicated boiler above their bath), which indicate an earlier consideration of problems that are still widespread and topical today, but have not yet been fully assimilated into the practice of design.   170   Georges Vigarello, *Le Propre et le Sale : L'hygiène du corps depuis le Moyen Âge* (Paris: Éditions du Seuil, 1987).   171   Katarzyna Marciniak, "Foreign women and toilets," *Feminist Media Studies* 8, no. 4 (Routledge, 2008): 337–356. Tara Atluri and Emily S. Davis, "The Intimacies of Globalization: Bodies and Borders On-Screen," *Camera Obscura* 62, vol. 21, no. 2 (Durham: Duke University Press, 2006): 33–73. On the relation between bathroom attendants, cleaners, racism and architecture and interior design see: "You Marxist, I Clean Toilets. Racism, Labor, and the Bathroom attendant," *FRAME: a journal of visual and material culture* 1 (Utrecht: Utrecth University, 2011): 69–95.

INTIMACY EXPOSED

INTIMACY EXPOSED

INTIMACY EXPOSED